Inner

A Guide to Peace and Empowerment

Andrew Da Passano
with Judith Plowden

Harper & Row, Publishers, San Francisco

Cambridge, Hagerstown, New York, Philadelphia, Washington
London, Mexico City, São Paulo, Singapore, Sydney

With special thanks to Julian Plowden for his keen editorial eye and talent for clarity;
To Virginia Da Passano, for loving support;
And to my students, who asked for this book.

FIRST EDITION

Library of Congress Cataloging-in-Publication Data

Da Passano, Andrew.
Inner silence.

1. Spiritual life. I. Plowden, Judith. II. Title.
BL624.D23 1987 291.4'48 87-45171
ISBN 0-06-250181-X (pbk.)

---

87 88 89 90 91 MPC 10 9 8 7 6 5 4 3 2 1

To my daughter Irene and my grandson Robert
with all my love

CONTENTS

The willing, Destiny guides them; the unwilling, Destiny drags them.

SENECA

BEYOND INNER NOISE

We make so much noise with our technology that we cannot discover that the stargate is in our foreheads.

WILLIAM IRWIN THOMPSON

Commune with your own heart, and in your chamber, and be still.

BOOK OF COMMON PRAYER

Silence is a healing for all ailments.

ANCIENT JEWISH PROVERB

The truth will present itself to the heart that is prepared for any possibility.

STEPHEN LEVINE

Working toward a transformation of consciousness is the only game in town.

BOB TOBEN

BEYOND INNER NOISE

I am happy you opened this book, because here I finally meet you. Hello! And I must also say, "come in!"—because as you open this book, you also open a door.

To what? Well, let's say to other worlds—or, if you prefer, to other dimensions. On this door is written "INNER SILENCE." Inner silence is the formula, the entry to the quantum leap—and I don't mean just theoretically, I mean practically.

Do you know how much noise we carry around inside us? Try a little experiment right now: Close your eyes. Tune out your surroundings and background noises, and focus on what's going on inside yourself. Breathe in a normal way. Listen for a minute. How many inner voices have you heard?

It will be the same story if you go to a cabin deep in the forest, hundreds of miles from the city. You are there to find peace, to restore and refresh yourself. You settle down, close your eyes, and listen—there is no traffic outside, only the soft roar of the wind through pine needles. "Ah," you think, "this is it." But no. The physical body, the emotions, the thoughts, are making a racket, clamoring for your attention. You have made a very interesting discovery: Even in the remarkably noisy age we live in, the real noise is inside.

The goal of this book is to help you to achieve inner silence—which will bring you not only "the peace that passes all understanding," but will also empower you to make changes in your life. Human life has one universal constant: It is *unpredictable.* What each one of us wishes is to have the power to control our own personal destiny so that we won't be at the mercy of all the ups and downs—especially the downs.

To acquire the rare powers born from inner silence, a certain discipline is required. Discipline is not a popular word. In our era, discipline connotes a reluctant obligation, something one must undertake through coercion. It is only in sports and competitive activities, which promise profit and stardom, that discipline is accepted in our culture. But that in itself is proof that only through discipline can outstanding achievements be expected.

This discipline I will offer you in two forms: explanations and techniques.

The explanations might really shake up your old ideas. As you read, you will throw out a lot of rubbish that has been stored in your mental attic. Stay with me: If you follow patiently along, the explanations will actually take you *beyond* the theories of today's quantum physicists.

As to the techniques, they have been known for thousands and thousands of years, but kept secret. When they were given out to a chosen few, they were dressed up in a lot of religious robes and turbans and other impressive ornaments. Stripped of their trappings, the techniques represent an accumulation of practical knowledge, tested in the most pragmatic way. They work—if they didn't, they wouldn't still be around.

It's quite simple, really. All human effort, all philosophies, and religions especially are based on the understanding and realization of two main issues: a better life, which means one that is long, happy, healthy, and acceptably prosperous; and, as the calendars inevitably pile up, our growing preoccupation with the continuity of our beloved "I" beyond the grave. All the rest is mere window dressing and escapism.

Please don't dismiss me as "too practical" a "spiritual" teacher. The blissed-out types aren't of much use to anybody, not even to themselves. I have written this book to give open-minded people a chance to fast-forward their destiny, to dump their obsolete software and make the quantum leap—not flattening their noses on a chalky blackboard, but leaping right through it into the multidimensional continuum. Far beyond dear old Albert's dreams.

"Beyond the quantum leap"—does it sound too much like magic? I've been saying for fifty years that science is the democratization of magic. Magic used to be for very few. To acquire magic takes years—it is an aristocracy of technicians. But nowadays you don't have to sit for decades in a monastic cell. A lot of the old dreams of magic are around us every day. If you don't believe it, let's look together.

Telepathy? We have the telephone. Just as quick and much more precise.

Walking on water? Levitation? Do you really want to walk three thousand miles to Paris? At 9 A.M. you can levitate with the Concorde in a comfortable armchair, enjoying breakfast; then eat your *dejeuner* at 1 P.M. at the Tour D'Argent in Paris; and be back at 6 P.M. for your cocktail at the Plaza.

Ubiquity—being in different places at once? Holograms can multiply your 3-D presence as many times as desired; and you have all the video cassettes in 2-D, and color and sound wherever you want.

All this magic has been provided by science—the only powers needed are cash or a credit card. And just as yesterday's magic is today's reality, the magic gadgetry of tomorrow is today's theoretical science.

Theoretical science constantly pushes back the outer envelope of the known world. The most advanced theories of quantum physics have prepared our minds for new possibilities. Physicists tell us that everything, even the most seemingly solid mountain, is in fact a vibrating field of energy. From this we can extrapolate that if all is energy in continual flux, then anything and everything is possible. This knowledge will help us greatly to attain inner silence, because it will stop our mind from constantly telling us, "It cannot be, therefore it isn't."

But to understand who leaps, how, and where, do not expect science to tell you. Too much ballast still hangs on official beliefs;

too much, in the name of conservatism, is fed into young minds. What I am offering today is not for yesterday's minds.

We can and must make the quantum leap now, and let official science catch up later. We need to change ourselves from Homo sapiens into the species of the future—you only have to look around you to see how urgently this is needed. To accelerate our own evolution, we need new software and this is what I hope to give you in this book.

THE WAY WE ARE

Because you still identify with the body-mind, you are lacking in true understanding.

NISARGADATTA

. . . they [the emotions and passions], ever restless, ever fighting for predominance, careless of harm or morals, turn the seeker's soul into a cage of monkeys.

FROM A PALI TEXT

I believe that in the overwhelming majority of individuals emotions are restrictive. The emotional responses are relatively primitive, powerful, reactive experiences that are understood poorly if they are understood at all.

W. BRUGH JOY, M.D.

We must vitalize the emotional body from within and send through it the emotions which we determine to have . . .

J. J. VAN DER LEEUW, L.L.D.

The mind of a yogi is under his control; he is not under the control of his mind.

SRI RAMAKRISHNA

Chapter 1

THE WAY WE ARE

To understand why there is so much inner noise, we need first of all to find out how a human being is constructed. The religions of the good old days told us that we had a body; then at death our soul—whatever that might be—jumped out, and grabbing its belongings, both dark and light, was rushed to a celestial courthouse. But it isn't as simple as all that. In fact we have three bodies—the physical, emotional, and mental vehicles—all operating at once.*

The Physical Vehicle

First of all, as everyone knows, we have the physical vehicle—the body. St. Francis of Assisi, with affection, called it Brother Donkey. Because of our sense of touch we think it is real, and we identify with it. We exercise great efforts to make it look as attractive as possible, and keep it from hurting. But St. Francis had the right idea: You need to treat Brother Donkey with loving attention, but it is not *you.* You live in it, but you are not it.

It may surprise you to learn that our "too, too solid flesh" really isn't. It is composed of atoms, little whirlwinds of energy. Atoms and their subatomic particles, the electrons, positrons, neutrinos,

* You may have heard of the etheric body. It is quite parenthetical to a basic description of a human being, but let us mention it for the sake of clarity. It lies between the physical and emotional bodies. It is not as subtle as the emotional, nor as gross as the physical. It is made of electromagnetic energy fields, which pass through the body as currents. Mostly ignored by Western medicine until recently, it functions through the meridians of oriental acupuncture and the *nadis* of Ayurvedic medicine in India.

quarks, are nothing we can see, grasp, divide, or weigh. Remember, the atom is not matter, it's a field of energy, as immaterial as the field you find between two magnets.

When atoms pool together, they create a molecule. And when the molecules throng together in our bodies they create a cell. And when the cells join together they create all the organs, which together make up the physical body.

The Emotional Vehicle

Next we have the emotional vehicle, just as real as the physical, but less cohesive, less condensed. The emotional body is finer, more subtle. It exists at the molecular level, like a mist, or like perfume. You can't see perfume, but it pervades everything, it can even go through the walls of a house. The emotional body interpenetrates the physical; it pervades every cell, makes things go, just as gasoline fuels the car, so to speak. The emotions make the organs function—to absorb, secrete, transmute, pass nutrients to other organs. It is emotion that makes the tiny cells perform—the leucocyte will jump on an invading microbe the way a cat contracts its muscles and pounces on a mouse. If the leucocyte didn't have emotions, it would just sit around and say, "Look at those fat microbes."

The entire scale of manifestation that constitutes a human being is moved about by the emotions, and this movement makes a lot of noise. The emotions, with all their power, are like a cage full of monkeys—and almost as impossible to control! If you step back and watch your own emotions with detachment, you will see that each is doing its own thing—leaping about, banging the trapeze, scratching, trying to fornicate, eating, swinging, whatever—and doing it constantly. And always *wanting* to do something.

This is the main characteristic of human emotions: They are out for kicks. They shun the unpleasant situation and rush for the pleasant one, whether they have to create it or ask for it or imagine it—emotions *must* vibrate, must be active. Nothing which is manifested wants to die, including an emotion. Sometimes we will even perpetuate an unpleasant emotion such as grief just to continue the vibration. A person may automatically watch the same bloody tragedy over and over again on the television news, even though there is no new information to be had — just to sustain the vibration.

The Mental Vehicle

Finally, we come to the mind — our mental vehicle. It is quite different from the other two. The mental body, more subtle than the emotional and physical bodies, is a series of electronic interactions that we have developed over our long evolution.

Hundreds of thousands of years ago, when we were still at the beginning, we were one with Nature. We simply flowed, as the animals do in the wild. Our little brothers, the animals, don't know why they have to mate, but they do know when. They don't know why they mustn't drink until the sun has set, but they don't do it. They are guided by "instincts," or what I call a "group soul." This group soul is a "mind" shared by all the members of the species. This group soul does not make mistakes; it simply gets on with its job in silence.

When we humans operated instinctively, we were okay. But as time passed our capacity to reason expanded. This capacity exists in the brain of every moving creature on Earth — it is by no means only a human privilege. But as we developed the unique power to visualize abstractions — to see in our minds something that never has been, something that might be in the future — our power to reason also grew. This development of abstract thought and visualization, and the practice of selection, decision, and action, led to an overgrowth or hypertrophy of reason. Reason began to take over our whole life process.

So what happened? As a defensive reaction, the instinct of the species retreated inside. It permeated the human metabolism in order to prevent emotions from manipulating Reason to obtain pleasurable sensations, thus saving humanity from premature destruction through its own foolish excesses. We call it the autonomic nervous system.

The autonomic nervous system functions on a totally occult level. Rationally, we have no idea what's going on, how much adrenaline we must squeeze into the veins, how many times we must accelerate our heartbeat, or take air into our lungs. We are permitted to live in this body, yet we do not know how to handle it. This instinct is virtually infallible. Left to its own devices, it never makes a mistake. Of course, it has organizational difficulties. When we humans take drugs, smoke, drive too fast, get all excited about everything, and stress and tire our organism, our metabolism has a hell of a time.

Reason is simply not capable of putting the monkey cage of emotions in order. Of course, some people are more reasonable than others, some more passion-directed. The point is that when we want to have a whiskey, then a second one, then a third, and Reason—which has its job to do—speaks up: "Stop it, stop it, you're going to kill yourself with this habit!" the emotions reply, "Ah, come on, you old spoilsport, I feel good for the first time in days, really good, and one more can't do me any harm." This is the way we function. We get ourselves in a lot of trouble and then say, "If only I had known . . ."

Certainly, it is quite difficult to control the emotional body. But proper awareness of how a human being is put together, coupled with inner preparation and empowerment through techniques, can enable us to handle stress and to deal with the unpredictability of our existence.

It is easy to envy the rich and famous who build themselves mansions on the tops of hills, overlooking the streets below where the noise and smog settle. But their lives are just as unpredictable and full of stress as the lives of ordinary people. The very fact of being rich and famous creates tension, ambitions, worries, preoccupations, plans which are constantly projected out of the present into a very improbable future. Rich or poor, our vehicles have the same composition—with the emotional body riding roughshod over the others.

Now Reason is a noble instrument, because it will help us on the path to wisdom. I suggest you make Reason your ally. But it is necessary to understand that it is like a computer—as they say, "Garbage in, garbage out." Reason has definite limitations, both in hardware and software. It lays its small grid of logic on the chaos produced by our sensory information, and only accepts that which fits its four categories of time, space, cause, and effect. These categories are *a priori*: before birth. They are part of the brain's blueprint. Anything outside of them—so-called paranormal events, or abstract concepts such as virtue or courage—Reason rejects as unreal. In this way, Reason is rather like a Newtonian physicist: If a thing can't be measured, weighed, quantified, then it can't be said to exist.

The Mind's Potential: Evolution

Reason has its limitations, but your mind has far greater capacities than you may realize. Science and technology have changed our lives—literally. We've been handling so much complex gadgetry lately that we have developed circuits in our brains that people thousands of years ago simply did not have. For instance, the ancient Greeks were not capable of perceiving as many colors as we can today—thus Homer called the blue Mediterranean "the wine-dark sea" because the perception of "blue" did not exist.

You have probably heard that we only use 10 percent to 14 percent of our brain. Have you wondered what the rest is for? It is there *for our future development*, for the evolution of our species.

But what is evolution?

Evolution is the complication of energy/matter: energy that we perceive as matter. Everything complicates itself as it develops in any new direction.

There are two kinds of evolution: You might call them horizontal and vertical. The horizontal hugs the earth, so to speak. It is a terrestrial affair. Horizontal evolution is a *functional* bettering of things in which moral values are not involved.

For example, let's take the bow and arrow. It first became a crossbow, then a machine gun, and finally an atom bomb. Is that bettering? Of course it is. The fundamental goal of a weapon like the bow and arrow is to kill—whether it be rabbits or your neighbor. As a bomb, it now kills much better, therefore it has evolved. It has become much more complicated.

Now, the other evolution is a vertical one, it reaches for the heavens. It is also a bettering, but in a different sense: The complicated, noisy energy which is at the root of the functioning of a human being is moving towards simplification. That is, it is moving toward its essence. It returns to its essence by shedding the useless. And as it sheds, along with simplification comes inner silence and peace.

Once we understand this vertical evolution and apply it to our physical manifestation on this three-dimensional level, then the energy of this vertical evolution can return to its essence. It will return pregnant with wisdom, unattached, totally serene, and finally free from the laws of constant return.

So this is the path you are traveling, and now you have seen how wonderfully complex you are. But who are *you* exactly? Who is it that rides in all these vehicles? It is consciousness, the sense of "I am," the awareness of "I." And it is this "I" who is going to control the inner noise.

CALMING THE VEHICLES

Behaviorist psychology . . . considers nothing real or true unless it can be verified by someone else's research. Buddhist psychology is precisely the opposite. Everything has to be verified by your own experience.

WALT ANDERSON

Once you have a meditative practice that suits you, you can do it most anywhere. You will find many ordinary moments in your life are perfect for meditation: when you are waiting in the dentist's office, or for the bus, or sitting on a subway. Moments which usually were times for boredom or wandering thoughts become a gift—a chance to meditate.

RAM DASS

Silence is the garden of meditation.

MAXIMS OF ALI

The practice of physical silence restores our body and sense organs. The practice of mental silence refreshes our mind and quickens all our inner faculties. The power gained through it is tremendous.

SWAMI PARAMANANDA

The most important point is to own your physical body. If you slump, you will lose your self. Your mind will be wandering about somewhere else; you will not be in your body.

SHUNUYU SUZUKI

Chapter 2

CALMING THE VEHICLES: MEDITATION AND REVERENCE

Now we must begin to calm the three vehicles. To do this I will give you some explanations and techniques. They may seem strange to you, but try them. Remember: You don't have to believe what I tell you. On the contrary, keep your critical capacity on its toes. In my schools I insist on one thing: Never believe what I tell you. Experiment for yourselves.

We all need evidences. What I can suggest to you, for example, might be excellent for you, but absolutely negative for your friend—one person's paté is another's poison. Therefore, when you accept some teaching, you may have a working hypothesis; but you have solved nothing, because the next fellow might tell you the contrary. However, when you have learned something for yourself, it is yours, a personal evidence. Nobody will take it away from you. This is extremely important; it will give you stability. So, experiment!

Preparing the Vehicle

Much can be done to improve our physical health and to achieve longevity. Most people eat far too much—we only get about 30 percent of our energy from food anyway. We lose much energy during digestion because of many factors; we rarely chew sufficiently—we seem to forget that our stomach has no teeth! We hope to be nourished by what is on the table, but we know most of the nourishment has been lost through overrefining, additives, and preservatives, and we have little choice in the matter.

I am not going to talk extensively about diets, but let me tell you that it is good sense when you follow one to see what it has done to the inventor. Look at his picture. If he looks like something you would not want to turn into, then you'd better find another diet. Generally speaking, a diet that is 50 percent grains and cereals is good for energy intake and healthy elimination, which is so important.

What about vegetarianism? Many of us are aware of the gory details of slaughterhouses, and have a repulsion against causing pain to innocent animals. So much has been said about it, there is no use going over the same ground. But I would like you to consider the following: The whole digestive tract of humans is much longer than that of other meat-eating animals. That is why the meat we consume gets trapped in the turnings of our intestines, where it decays for days. This is the cause of many cases of constipation, colonic disorders, and blood pollution with its consequence of halitosis. Fish, however, being of a softer texture, is more easily digested and eliminated.

During its evolution, every manifested being, knowingly or not, is in the cosmic thrust towards liberation. All manifestation is moving toward Light, that is, towards the transcendence of form. Forms and shapes are limitations of energy. You can see this by the mere fact that a form has an outer limit—otherwise, it would be amorphic, formless. The animal group souls, which direct each particular species through the inner impulses we call instinct, have each one chosen according to its characteristics, a path toward this goal. Some, like our pets, chose love. Through love's exchange, each one evolves toward a higher manifestation, imitating its human master. Some, like horses, chose the way of service. Luckily, their martyrdom is almost terminated—they have accomplished their goal. Others, like cattle, go through the lengthy path of being assimilated as food into a more evolved entity like the human being.

So, as you consume the flesh of animals, be conscious of their sacrifice—from the Latin *sacrum facere,* to do something sacred. If when you eat, you are fully aware of your action, your reverential attitude will dissolve the negative elements of the animal's fear and pain.

Here is another vitally important point about diet: The human constitution is divided into positive and negative energy—*yang* and *yin*. Although men tend to be *yang* and women *yin*, each individual, independent of gender, has more of one than the other. Food follows the same law. Some *yin* foods taken in excessive quantity, fruit for instance, will create an imbalance in the metabolism. Western medicine has no understanding of this, and if a doctor advises a fruit diet to a person who is already strongly *yin*, it will create a catastrophic situation. Only through a thorough knowledge of acupuncture and Ayurvedic medicine can the physical effects of food be traced and controlled. Even the excesses of vegetarianism can sometimes have negative effects. Have you noticed that most of the Hindu gurus through the centuries have been bald?

Moderation in food and adequate exercise will help to prepare your physical vehicle for the experience of inner silence, and for passing through that door to all the possibilities beyond.

Meditation: The Subdivision of the Bodies

I hope you do not have a built-in resistance to the idea of meditation because it has come to us from the East. In fact, meditation was very well known in the early Christian church, and has been used throughout the centuries in contemplative orders such as the Trappists. It is gradually—almost gingerly—being introduced into a few Protestant branches. Meditation is the basic tradition in all the East, from the Sufis of Islam to the students of the Jewish Qabbala. Around the world, hundreds of millions of people are meditating every day.

There are countless systems of meditation. But whatever the

system, this process of centering, of calm awareness in inner silence, becomes a way of life. Most meditation techniques are good, although some are too oriental for us—we busy Westerners cannot easily give several hours every morning to achieve serenity.

I never lived in a monastery—I had a wife, a family, and professional obligations, with precise dates of delivery for my artwork. So I had to find means suitable for Westerners. After years of research I chose the Tibetan Buddhist system, because it was faster and to the point.

The Subdivision of the Bodies

In the tradition we shall share, correct meditation begins with *concentration*. This becomes the second level, *meditation*, which in turn leads to the third level, *contemplation*.

The word contemplation doesn't mean much to us in the West. It is nothing anyway but an accepted translation, and a bad one. It transmits a sense of passive monastic beatitude, and so is often repulsive to active people. In fact, it is quite the opposite. Contemplation is a state that permits us to synthesize, not analyze, simultaneous knowledge. You receive the total truth, in one piece. You *know*, and that's all. It's not an intellectual process, it clearly comes from somewhere else.

The technique I give you to control our three vehicles in meditation actually divides them. It is called the Subdivision of the Bodies. Our physical, emotional, and mental bodies interact constantly, giving us the impression of a unity, the *individuus*—the one that cannot be separated. But the unity can indeed be divided, if you know how, in order to leave our mental vehicle capable of serene, quiet thinking: by stopping the other ones from hassling it all the time.

First of all, the physical body must enter into complete relaxation. It is a totally relaxed, cataleptic state, without rigidity. The physical body must be completely forgotten. The body, the surroundings, the interaction of surroundings with the body must be dissolved. Yes, it is possible. Have you ever been bitten by an insect during the night, only to discover it in the morning? The bite did not wake you up, because your consciousness was not on the physical level during those hours. As we mentally dissolve the physical body, we close the entries to the five senses as well. Think of how it is when you are totally engrossed in a wonderful book. You are not conscious of anything else, of aches in your back, the smell of cooking from the kitchen, or noises in the next room. The only reality for a while is that book.

Now, the emotional body is also called the *astral* body. It has a molecular density. Like water, it can be as subtle as mist, or as invisible as humidity. Therefore we can freeze this astral—it'll keep quiet. No noisy vibrations; winds blowing on a frozen lake cannot create waves.

We need to understand that the astral/emotional body obeys its own laws. Everything that you visualize on your mindscreen reflects in the astral. The astral has no more autonomy to refuse to reflect the image than electricity can refuse to follow a wire.

Therefore, the physical body cannot be controlled if the astral body has an inkling of the possibility of moving the energy through the nerves. The astral body will do everything it can (because it loves to vibrate) to move the physical body, throwing the meditator off balance. But, since it has to respond to our visualization, we can freeze it into serenity.

As for the mind, we will first observe it peacefully, then we will be giving it something to do. Here's the technique:

First, find a place where you will be undisturbed. Sit on the floor, on a rug or cushion if you can, and cross your legs tailor-fashion. This traditional attitude of meditation will keep your body relaxed but alert, and your spine straight. If you feel uncomfortable at the joints—knees and ankles—sit on a higher cushion or a small stool. If your physical condition does not permit you to sit on the floor, it is perfectly all right to use a straight-backed chair. (This is called the Egyptian position.) It is better if you do not cross your ankles, but keep both feet on the floor.

Do not lie down. You don't want to go to sleep and miss the

whole show! But once you are used to meditating, you can occasionally sit propped up in bed with pillows—as long as you are awake and alert.

I suggest you use the same place, the same corner, for each meditation. The area will gradually become imbued with your own peaceful energy, and just being there will help you to calm yourself. You might want to add a small table or shelves with a candle, flowers, and incense. These are optional frills, but they do help to create the mood, to set the stage.

Now breathe deeply several times, preparing the body to relax. You are letting your body know this is a special time. Breathe from the diaphragm—it expands as you inhale, lifting the air up into your lungs, and becomes concave as you exhale. Breathe gently and slowly.

When you are fully relaxed, the next step is to "dissolve" the physical body by taking away the energy. Start at the tips of your toes and sense/feel/visualize that you are drawing energy up the feet to the ankles; then toward the knees; then into the thighs. Do this until both legs are thoroughly relaxed. Next, lift the energy from your fingertips into your hands, up your arms to the elbows, and slowly up to your shoulders. Hands and arms are relaxed. Now the energy comes up from the buttocks, up the torso. (It may help to visualize this as the water level rising in a tank.) The energy leaves the stomach; goes up the chest; and up to the throat, which swallows once. All the muscles of the neck relax. The muscles around the mouth go slack. The brow is smooth, free of tension.

Imagine your physical energy going out through a small opening at the very top of your head—where the soft spot on a baby is found. This is the crown *chakra*. *Chakra* is the Sanskrit word for a center of psychic energy. We have as yet no word for it in English.*

---

* The root *chakra*, the *muladhara*, is at the base of the spine. The second *chakra*, the *swadhistana*, is below the navel and called the *chi* by the Chinese. The third subtle energy center, at the solar plexus, is the *manipura*. *Anahata* is the name of the heart *chakra*, in the center of the chest. At the throat is found the *vishudda*, and between the brows is the *ajna chakra*, or "third eye." When these six are developed, the seventh appears—the crown *chakra* or *sahasrara*, also known as the thousand-petaled lotus.

Next imagine that your body is heavy, as heavy as lead. Feel it as a lead statue. You have taken all the energy out of your physical body. Your body is totally still.

Now think/feel/visualize in your mind that your body is made of white wax, like candle wax. Feel it as wax, feel the texture, sense/see the color. Then realize that you are not a solid body of wax at all but a thin film of wax, like a coated candle. Like a candle statue of Buddha. Feel very light, almost buoyant.

(Do not be concerned about the "meaning" of these images. They are deliberately irrational. We have to get around Reason, remember?)

Then imagine under the hollow white wax a bed of red, flaming coals, as in a forge. The wax starts to melt, becoming a cloud of whitish smoke. The physical body is gone. We are now left with our emotional or astral body. It is like a body of mist, like a snowman made of mist, with no clear features and slightly larger than our physical body.

This is the astral body of emotions—so difficult to calm down and control. But control it we shall. See the whitish blue of the astral body become a deeper and deeper blue, like ice; a cold frozen blue like the folds of the snow when the sun has set. Now assert to yourself: "My astral body is frozen. Relaxed and serene. All my emotions are *totally* turned off, all my emotions are now extinguished; my astral body is now frozen."

Say this to yourself two or three times until you really feel it is so.

As soon as you visualize the blue color of the astral body, lift your attention to a point between the eyebrows, the sixth *chakra*, the third eye. You are in the mental body. See a large, golden disc. Think/feel/see it. (Visualization is harder for some people than others. But don't try to actually *see* it on your closed eyelids. Think it, feel it, imagine yourself in it. With diligent practice it will become easier.)

Assert: "I am in my mental body. My mental body is totally relaxed." Immediately see the word PEACE appear on the golden disc in large, black block letters. See each letter individually, and the word as a whole. Hold it.

For the beginning weeks of meditation, hold onto that word and simply observe that there is no activity of your mind. If random thoughts come, watch them drift by like clouds in the sky. The clouds come and go, the sky remains. If a train of thought should take you away for a few seconds, when you catch yourself simply come back. Restore the disc and the word PEACE.

When you have enjoyed a refreshing time in peace and inner silence, end this meditative practice by restoring energy to all three bodies in the form of golden light. Gold is a healing color, a symbol of vigor. To do this, reverse the process. See the golden disc without the word. Come to your astral body and fill it with golden light, from the head down. Then experience your physical body as you are sitting. As you take a deep breath, fill it too with golden light. Now when you open your eyes you feel strong, confident, and healthy.

Though there may seem to be many steps and images to this technique, do not be discouraged. Read through the instructions twice before you undertake the process, and refer back to the directions if you have to. The next day it will seem more natural, and in a few days it will unfold effortlessly.

After three or four weeks it will be time to move deeper into the silence of meditation. Rightful meditation is sinking into total silence. Silence of the senses, silence of inner muscular tone, silence of feeling.

The more advanced processes of concentration, meditation, and contemplation will be given in chapter 5. For now, I suggest you work with the Subdivision of the Bodies. It's a bit like learning to play the piano. You don't start out with concertos, you simply practice scales. This beginning meditation may be like practicing the scales, but it has nothing of that tedious quality. Soon you will have a control over your three vehicles that will develop into a mastery.

The best time for meditation is in the very early morning. All other times are important, but this is the best moment. Its benefits should spread like a golden light over your whole day.

Reverence

One attitude, one feeling, one condition is absolutely necessary for meditation, and that is *reverence.* The state of reverence in meditation will go beyond Reason to a new perception. It is a foretaste of inner silence. It is love without a fixed point, love without a goal or target. It is religiousness without idols.

How do you find this state, which is your center? Try looking into your past. See if there is something in your youth to evoke in memory—hymns, "Ave Maria," candles and incense, prayers, an empty church or temple—recreate these elements, these moments, if they trigger the state of reverence in you. Listen to tapes of religious music—perhaps of monks singing Gregorian chants—and try to blend in with the ritual, hear their clarity of love and devotion. Devotion may not be your tendency, but you can use the thrust of devotion in others which has accumulated through time. You can have reverence for reverence itself.

If no childhood memory works for you, then imagine the great starry night sky, the vast heavens overhead with millions of stars and galaxies. Better still, experience the brilliant night sky in the desert, far from the lights of the city. You should have a feeling of awe, of yielding, with love and trust, to something greater, something to which you aspire. This is reverence. Deep compassion is born from it, and it opens the doors to all your possibilities.

Now, from techniques back to explanations—perhaps even an explanation of why you are reading this book.

HOW WE CREATE OUR WORLD

The exploration of the atomic and subatomic world in the twentieth century has revealed an unsuspected limitation of classical ideas, and has necessitated a radical revision of many of our basic concepts.

FRITJOF CAPRA

Our normal waking consciousness . . . is but one special type of consciousness, whilst all about it, parted from it by the flimsiest of screens, there lie potential forms of consciousness entirely different.

WILLIAM JAMES

Sorcerers say that we are inside a bubble. It is a bubble into which we are placed at the moment of our birth. At first the bubble is open, but then it begins to close until it has sealed us in. That bubble is our perception. We live inside that bubble all our lives. And what we witness on its round walls is our own reflection.

CARLOS CASTANEDA

All the world's a stage.

WILLIAM SHAKESPEARE

We have dreamt the world as firm, mysterious, visible, ubiquitous in space and durable in time; but in its architecture we have allowed tenuous and eternal crevices of unreason which tells us it is false.

JORGE LUIS BORGES

Chapter 3

HOW WE CREATE OUR WORLD

One day we suddenly awake to the necessity of modifying our life, to the feeling that we are the victim of some sort of destiny, or whatever we call it. This really is a flash of rebellion, and it comes from a certain level of maturity, reached through the accumulation of life's experiences. The worse they are, the faster the rebellion.

But when we start trying to modify the world around us, we discover it is nearly impossible, for the world is already set in its ways. Then the questions arise: "Why was I born? Where did I come from? What the hell am I doing here? What is going to happen to me during the rest of my life and . . . after?" To ask the first "why" is to take the first step on the path to wisdom.

The Illusion of the Senses

Now we are going to deal with the illusion of the senses. Stick with me. It may require some effort on your part, but you've got to absorb this.

If we turn to Reason for answers to the "whys," we will become restless and frustrated. When we ask "why," we begin to question the dimensions beyond Reason's reach, yet we find we are limited to using the same old measuring tools—time, space, cause, effect. This is what happens in traditional science. It will always tell you how, and how much, and when, but rarely can it tell you why. Our computer, Reason, receives its data *only* through the five senses, and so denies all validity to anything which does not comply with its rules. And this denial is an obstacle to our development.

I do not want to belittle our rational computer. On the contrary, I recognize its values and through my explanations try to make an ally of Reason. I believe that I have, through my forty-five years of teaching, succeeded in doing so. But, nevertheless, Reason has its limits. And when a machine has its limits, so has its output.

The world is perceived by each of us in a given way according to our own construct, our own values, our own personality. Nothing in it can be modified without adequate understanding and without adequate techniques. So first let's take a look at the ways in which we are the creators of our world.

Sound

Since this book is about silence, we'll begin with sound. Is there any sound?

No. Of course, as children we learned differently. We learned that when you hit a gong, the sound waves hit your ears and go to your brain. But this is sheer nonsense. I don't know why it's easier to teach a lie than a truth, but that's the way things go in our noisy civilization.

Here is what really happens: All objects on this planet are immersed in air. When I hit a gong, the ripples of air—the air in which the gong is vibrating—go to the ears. There they meet a rather complicated paraphernalia—the ear drum, the cochlea, the little hammer, the little stirrup. The air ripples run around there for a while before reaching a nerve, the eighth cranial nerve that goes up to the brain, where they sort of tickle the circuits of our brain construct. At that moment the airwaves become sound. Before, there are no sound waves at all. If you are on the moon you can beat a gong until your arm aches, but nothing will happen. Why? Because there are no air ripples to hit your ears, and therefore there is no possibility of hearing a sound.

When a great cellist gives a concert, what he or she really does is to use horse-tail stretched on a bow to scratch dried cat's intestines stretched over a wooden box. This sends out air ripples that enter into our ears and transmit signals to our brains. It enthralls us and, believe it or not, it can even change the spiritual tone of an audience.

We organized music through the centuries by considering some of the tickling sensations as high notes, some others as medium or low notes—some pleasant, some screeching, some soft. And when these are well balanced through the scratching of the cat's guts, everybody is extremely happy.

So, alas, poor Wolfgang, poor Ludwig, no real music anywhere.

That's it, folks. No noise, no sound, utter silence. All the thunders, and voices, and music, and loving whispers never existed as such anywhere at any time. *Because we and only we, in our minds, are the creators of the sound and of our world.*

This statement would have been totally unacceptable to the old obsolete vision of science. But it is the root of empowerment, the basis for the transmutation of your life, for destiny present and future. Let us not think it preposterous. It stands as a basic biblical affirmation—the oldest story in town—that we are made in the image of our Creator! Therefore we are creators; no more, no less.

Or are we supposed to believe that our "image" is to be limited to four limbs? Plus nose and ears? If the Divinity had indeed been made in this limited human way, would he not be a very poor Divinity indeed? In its craving for objectivity, this is what the human mind has done. We have reversed the biblical statement (which, by the way, was correct); and, in our anthropomorphic mania, we have made the Divinity into an idol, something we were specifically cautioned against.

Sight

What about sight? The first thing you see is the wall in front of you. But you can't see the surface without seeing color. It is the difference between the colors, or tones, of surfaces that gives you the size and shapes of objects in space.

How do we perceive what we call "color"? We can see no color in total darkness. The energy we call light (which has weight that can be measured through impact) hits a given object called X. We can see nothing of X until light strikes it. This X can absorb a certain quantity of light energy (photons)—so much and no more. Certain objects are voracious, keeping so much light energy that they heat up, giving back little. We then receive back on our retinas so little of light energy that we hardly perceive the colored surfaces of these objects, so we call them "dark." Other objects generously give back almost all the impact of the photons, and we receive the impact on our eyes as a blinding shock—sun's reflection on snow, for instance. The different grades of absorption of each of the objects around us create the various hues of our colorful world.

What can we learn from this? The first evidence we obtain through this analysis is that *we never see the object itself,* or its essence, but always and only the "bouncing-back" portion of light that has not been absorbed. The next evidence is that we can perceive only that bounced-back light which our eyes are capable of perceiving. For example, infrared or ultraviolet rays are not directly visible to our eyes; so in an apparatus or photo they are translated into a grey or green tone. We only see that which an object's characteristic quality of absorption permits us to see; and that bouncing-back quantity is reduced by our natural limitation to perceive a more extended chromatic scale. We only see the color the object *isn't!*

The good-old philologists of the eighteenth century translated the Sanskrit word *maya* as "illusion." But now you can grasp what is meant by illusion—the illusion that we see the total world as it is, while indeed we humans only perceive a very small proportion of the world's reality—our own limited view.

You will hear the word "limitation" repeatedly from me. By limitations is meant whatever our five senses can let us perceive of the cosmos around us. Reason puts in order the stimuli received by our senses from the chaos out there. All we can ever learn must constantly pass through this frame of reference.

This chaos is horrifying to Reason. Through this fear of the void we began, as condensed entities, through all the evolution of our species, to create the *bulwark of the senses,* which developed gradually to the present point of detail and precision, and forms a sort of bubble that we live in. Really we are enclosed in a bubble lined with mirrors, a bubble formed by our perceptive limits, and we float inside it, in the void. All intrusions from "out there" through cracks in our sphere seem frightening, "paranormal," "spooky."

Touch

Our most primitive sense is touch. Even more than sight, it is our most important evidence-giving sense. Whenever we are in doubt about anything, we extend our hand and get the feeling of something solid to grasp, something reassuring, something we can finally call "real." This habit has grown into an automatic reflex—people say, "I believe what I can see and touch."

Suppose you're "touching" a cement wall. Nothing is more real or objective to our senses, is it? What is really happening? The wall, of whatever material, is in essence composed of atoms. But what is an atom? We are told it consists of a nucleus, or center, and gravitating around it like a small solar system are electrons. The variation in number of these determines the matter under observation.

But neither the nucleus nor the electrons are "matter" in the popular sense. By matter, we naturally mean something solid; and a "material" atom is to our mind a little grain of something infinitely small, like a microscopic grain of sand. On the contrary, atoms are nothing more or less than fields of energy.

These small whirlwinds of energy are held together by a force we may call "cohesion," the intensity of which determines the characteristic of matter as we know it. In the case of the cement wall we have a cohesion factor of, let's say, 200. It comes in contact with a pickaxe of tempered steel, which we will say has a cohesion factor of 500. Charging the pickaxe with still more energy, that of impact, we may deduce that the matter of more cohesion will penetrate the weaker field and thus perforate the wall.

Our next deduction will nevertheless be that our sense of touch, so realistic and reassuring, is nothing more than another sensory illusion of reality. We may never contact, in any possible way, the essence of what we call a cement wall. We may at best oppose one field of energetic cohesion (weaker or stronger) to another, thus creating (by transmissions along our nerve cells to our brain) the sensation of solidity. Or, in the case of our hand versus air pressure or water, the sensation of softness and weakness of matter.

Remember that in neither case have we met with anything other than our own perceptual limitations. This is why we say our bubble is lined with mirrors—we always perceive what we are. The essence of X is still an X—and will always, on our human level, remain as such. Kant postulated this state of things when he said, "All transcendence is impossible to our human state, because ever, the Noumenon, by human cognition, is transformed into phenomenon."

Taste and Smell

For taste and smell, the principle is identical. Taste is the elaboration of messages sent to the brain through the nervous system by our tongue's papillae. They in turn receive sensations produced by chemical processes of the mixture of saliva with particles of an X. That X we "see" and "feel" or even "hear" (the bite of an apple, for example), but we do not know it *essentially*. Smell is an elaboration of particles brought into contact with the moist mucosa of the nasal system, very much like taste.

Creating Our World with Concepts

Each message brought to us by each separate sense organ is totally isolated and has no similitude whatsoever with any other. It takes a certain amount of time and effort to understand this fully.

When I hear for the first time a noise produced by percussion on an object unknown to me, I cannot deduce from that its shape, color, taste, or smell. Likewise, the color of an object I have never seen will never give me a hint as to its smell, hardness or taste.

You may say that if you see the color of an apple you can deduce approximately its hardness and taste. Yes, and that brings us to the next point. The objectivity of this world is built of the mental construction we call "concepts," brought about by deductions from acquired sensory experience: *memory*. We know from experience that green apples are sour and hard. We know a hollow box of wood gives forth a hollow sound, and that strings stretched over it on a small wooden bridge can produce what we call "deductively" a violin sound or guitar sound.

This is like building a room on a stage. With the erection of every wall, the scene becomes more and more "real." By adding the ceiling, we add the final touch to a thing which corresponds to our idea of a room. The more "roomy" details we add—lamps, windows, doors—the more the room becomes real.

Let's create an experience together: We see on a table a small, white cube. It seems rough. We suppose it to be a lump of sugar. All right, then, let's prove it. It will become sugar if all the elements we associate with the concept "sugar" are present. So we touch it. Yes, it's hard. It's also rough—but is it sweet? If it is, then our concept work is at an end, it's sugar. If the lump on the table lacks sweetness, then it falls into another category of objects, another concept—a piece of rough marble, for instance. Until we found an explanation for its existence (a piece of a building game, a practical joke, etc.) our mind would not rest. Reason would insist on placing it in a defined category.

We live, therefore, in a world where objects perceived in a limited way by our limited senses give us the illusion of being the total reality. In fact, they act like icebergs—the part perceived by our senses is just a portion of what we cannot perceive, which remains under the water line of our scale of observation. *We do not perceive the totality, let alone the essence.*

Furthermore, when we communicate between ourselves, we exchange concepts. When I say I will give you an apple, you don't really know what I will give you until I define the color, age, size, taste. With every added "concept," my apple will appear more and more real in your mind. But is my idea of "red" your idea of "red?" "Sweet?" "Big?" You must refer to comparison, that is, to your sensorial experience. So even precise definition is always approximate.

If a ten-year-old boy in Scotland describes a "big butterfly," is it the same "big butterfly" of a ten-year-old Brazilian boy?

This brings us to another step in the subjectiveness of our universe. To consider something as real, we need to have cooperation of the majority. If I see a flowerpot on a table, and the dozen people present declare in a definitive way that there is no flowerpot there, however apparent to my five senses the flowerpot may be, I will have doubts about its reality. I will then qualify the flowerpot as "real to me," but subjective—something like a dream which I cannot deny, but still cannot classify as "real."

Perhaps it is time for a moment of reassurance. Although I keep telling you that our Reason and our five senses are limited, they are still absolutely vital to our survival. They have evolved over millions of years, from the earliest blind, wormlike beginnings. They were indispensable for our evolving consciousness, aroused from the deep sleep of nature. Imagine our primitive self, groping out there in the darkness of the void. After the sense of touch, we started with "seeing spots," like the ivy plant has, and then we created more and more refined instruments that could finally be affected by the bouncing back of photons of light from objects to the eyes. As for Reason's limitations, they allowed the newborn brain to categorize, catalogue, differentiate the various stimuli that came in from the chaos of the cosmic immensity. A rational intelligence would be lost without coordinates and frames of reference; no event could ever become an experience, no experience could ever be treasured in the memory bank in the chaos of irrational, endlessly exploding events.

So, through cautious translations of what is out there, using our five senses and their elaboration in the mind, we have constructed reality. We take each new perception as real, thus setting up a conditioning that reinforces the illusion.

A Meditation on the Senses

Let us end this difficult chapter with a theme for you to meditate upon. Instead of staying with the golden disc and the word PEACE, think about the following sentences, turning them over and over in your mind, following where they lead: "There is no sound. There are no noises. Only vibrations of air that reach my ear. I translate these vibrations, put value on them, elaborate them in my brain. I am the creator of music, sighs, cries, yells, bells. All sound. What an extraordinary brain I have! But I am not the brain, it is but my instrument . . ."

EMPOWERMENT

Earth people always knew the world was round, and everything a circle. But if a white man doesn't discover something, there's nothing there.

GRANDFATHER BLACK ELK (LAKOTA)

The cosmos is a polarized field of forces that are constantly in the process of swirling into form and dissolving back into pure energy.

STARHAWK

The world of mental formulations set in motion by the contact-stimulus is the world in which we live. To say that it is not *real* does not mean that it is devoid of *existence.*

ALEXANDRA DAVID-NEEL

I'm always reluctant to use the word, God, because everybody seems to carry around his own stagnant images and definitions that totally cloud the ability to step outside a narrow, individual frame of reference. If we have any conception of what God is, certainly it should be changing and expanding as we ourselves grow and change.

BERNADETTE ROBERTS

You live in illusion and the appearance of things. There *is* a reality. You are that reality. When you realize this you will see that you are nothing, and being nothing, you are everything. That is all.

KALU RINPOCHE

Chapter 4

EMPOWERMENT

A few hundred years ago Europeans, including such great minds as Leonardo da Vinci and St. Thomas Aquinas, still believed the Earth was flat. You may smile at such childish ignorance, but beware—as you shall see, we are not much brighter today than they were then. In that epoch there was no reason to believe that the five senses were not reliable. Our electronic gadgetry didn't exist, and no one had ever displaced his body faster than a galloping horse could run. A flat Earth was therefore an absolute fact; and everybody from serf to king arranged his politics, economics, love life, and social activities according to this evidence. It was totally confirmed by popes and Bible-preachers, just like many other famous "evidences" we hear today. Doubting any of this was sin, and would only lead you down to the grill room.

The flat Earth was a dangerous superstition, because people were unaware of the abundance of food crops growing on the other side of the round earth. All they had in their fields to eat was turnips, carrots, beetroot, and grains. After a series of terrible winters and summers there were great famines, and hundreds of thousands died. Desperate, they took to grinding the bones of the dead to make flour for bread. The memory of this still survives as "Pan de Muertos" in Hispanic countries. In the rest of the world was everything they needed; but because of one erroneous thought form—the world being flat—nobody would go over the edge. So they starved.

Well, you can say, "What has all that to do with us?" Plenty. We are making the same kind of mistake. Since Columbus, we have developed an amazing technology. We certainly "fly faster than the arrow from the Tartar's bow"; we go to the moon and back; our communications systems are unique; we are great, we are conquerors. Quite a developed mammal indeed! But even though quantum physics shows us perfectly clearly that the material world doesn't exist, we still follow the tired old schooling of the past. Billions of people continue to think everything is matter—that atoms, however tiny, contain some fundamental particle that is solid.

This type of thinking is totally obsolete. We might just as well go around with white wigs and tap snuff boxes. We are stuck in a belief system which, because of its limitations, reduces our world vision to imaginary parameters—slightly more ample than the flat Earth version, but still totally unreal.

You may say, "Okay, so what? How can an obsolete opinion have an important effect on everyday life, work, relationships, and international politics?" You'll see—you'll see as you read on.

Trying to apply old ideas to reality is like trying to put square pegs into round holes. Fools don't understand—they get very angry, they go get a big hammer, and go on banging until the whole thing blows up in smoke. This is the way most people handle the situation. And it all might end very dramatically, as you know.

Just to make the Old Beards happy for once, let us call this cosmic energy field "energy/matter"—which really means energy that we, as we perceive it, translate as "matter." The only difference with the old vision is that "we" know matter is not only what it seems, and we have the agility to walk an open road. But "they" didn't—and still do not even today! They are stuck in a cul de sac.

Since the world is therefore composed of energy/matter at different grades of cohesion, then the Rock of Gibraltar is made of the same stuff as the dreams of a tender teenager. I would like you to think about this.

Cosmic Nuts and Bolts

So, we all act according to our evidences. For instance we can walk on ice, but we refuse to walk on thin ice. If we think that we are encased in a world of solids, we deduce a quantity of consequences and act accordingly. If our walls are of cement, even in case of emergency it's no use to push them. Now, the old view of the world made solid matter evident because it was and is so to our five senses—we had no reason to doubt them. We deduced everything from these senses. Therefore we considered it evident that we were this person that began, grew, and ended—this evidence focused our whole life on that which we called reality. As it then became evident, any happening beyond this state—sentiments, thoughts—though undeniably present in life, did not belong to solid reality. We called them subjective, not real or objective; they were not measurable.

And here our drama begins. It became the intelligent thing to push aside (as dispensable, as an epiphenomenon or side effect of "real" circumstances) everything that Reason did not consider real. This habit multiplied socially, politically, and internationally, without giving value to or taking into consideration what we *now* know to be the real values and needs of life. This kind of philosophy was called materialism.

In materialism people move forward motivated totally by fear—fear of lacking power to possess, fear of our own weakness and death, because we believe we only have the perceivable world at our disposal, after which we die and everything ends. This vision of reality isolates us from others. We feel we are not responsible, therefore we never consider ourselves involved. To avoid pain we remain voluntarily blind to the needs of life around us. This belief system has turned our social and political world into what we know it to be—a time bomb!

But why do I say a time bomb? Because the general public can see no connection between development of consciousness and a nuclear war. Although terrorized by the vision of the world holocaust, they get irritated at the mere idea of losing valuable time in such abstract and useless (for them) activities as meditation and expansion of consciousness. They prefer to throw themselves into endless international bickering in which they confront each other on the same primitive level, and it only funnels them toward the inevitable end. If those in charge could understand and enter other dimensions, the sense of cosmic unity could make them see that resorting to total destruction to solve commercial problems is like chopping off one's foot because one's shoe is muddy. There is an immensely great urgency for the new generation to increase awareness. Only by entering through the door of inner silence shall they become the new leaders who will take over the wheel before the old fools blow up the ship.

That is why it is necessary to understand the mechanics of our relation to the world around us, and not mistake our sensory perceptions for the only reality. In the East, the most considered discipline leading to the cosmic expansion of consciousness is Jnana Yoga, or union through understanding. The famous "third eye" dissolves the illusion of the senses and isolates for analysis the various combinations processed by our rational computer. It develops in the Jnana Yogin a clearer perception of the fastest cosmic frequencies, thus uniting simultaneously the reception of holistic evidences with the dissolution of illusions.

Their saying is, "The Jnana Yogin dissolves the world." To which any normal person objects: "I don't see how you can dissolve my refrigerator."

"Ah," replies the Yogin, "but I am not responsible for your hallucinations."

Do you get the joke?

Years ago, when I was a student of inner development, my master was Tulio Castellani, known as "The Venetian." After the class had worked for several months on understanding and experimenting with the nonexistence of objectivity, the nonreality of this world, and the nonexistence of matter, Tulio pulled some tricks on us to test our capacity. One day he told us: "I know that after all this hard work you have done you are perfectly aware of the energy structure of the world, and that matter is nonexistent as such. Would you please explain, as if to some young pupil, and also write it down, the following: I am driving my car. For some unfortunate reason I make an abrupt turn to the right, on the highway. I hit a motorcycle policeman, demolish his bike, send him to the hospital. I get handcuffed and land in jail! How can all this happen if this world is an illusion and matter doesn't exist? How does this work?"

Then my master also gave us another tough nut to crack: "Now that you have understood that time and space do not exist *per se*, but are only mental categories, I want you to write a paper which will explain—or, better said, will formulate, enumerate—in the format of our daily life, the mechanics of this happening. You now know that time and space do not exist. That's fine. But when you go from one town to another the landscape changes, and when you get there it is almost dark—how can this be? It should all remain 'as is,' don't you think? I'm expecting your papers next week. Good night!"

This gave me a terrible shock. It was as if all I had learned had suddenly collapsed, and all these years of work had turned into a pitiless farce. Some students came to see me and talk about it. They had clearly lost their footing and couldn't handle this at all. A couple of them, shaken to the core, left the Center for good.

I was then acquiring my mastery of Jnana Yoga, the purest and hardest of all Yogas. I worked at this assignment nonstop. For that week, my master had instructed me to take daily a couple of pills of glutamic acid as a brain booster, and bars of dark chocolate. All of this I did. He must have been right, as I finally achieved some interesting breakthroughs.

Now, I am a tender teacher. I don't want you to suffer any more—besides, my publisher instructed me to love my readers. So later in this same chapter you will find the solution to both questions. But if I were a Zen master, I would let my students sit there for hours, hitting them regularly on the head with a long bamboo stick, until they had discovered the right solutions. So you see how lucky you are to have me!

You may have noticed that the word "reality" is beginning to lose its solidity. It now appears more like a coin—on one side, reality, on the other, relativity. Because the change of atomic cohesion of each of these "realities" makes them very relative to each other. As we proceed, the stifling atmosphere of "material reality" will slowly give way before a wind of freedom. Something is changing.

By now you understand that the cosmic stimuli which we receive, we translate between our ears with our brain and its rational computer. These stimuli are all vibrations—the vibrations of energy fields. The cosmos vibrates. We translate these vibrations as a radio translates electrical impulses into air vibrations, and we again translate them into sound inside our brain. But what we illustrate on our mindscreen has nothing to do with the stimulus received by our sense terminals. *Nothing of what we perceive is as we perceive it.* No impulse ever has a form. We construct form from different impulses coming from different senses put together like one puts up a stage set. We live in a formless world. It is all waves, all vibrations.

If the world around us was indeed the way we think it is, we would never perceive anything. Why? Because our senses only respond to vibrations. "Music" is sound vibrations, selected and categorized. "Objects" are visible only because light photons bounce back and define shapes in space and colors the object sends back. When we contact the "objects," the opposition of their cohesions to our bodily cohesions we call "touch." We process messages that are formless, give them color, bulk, sound, shape inside our brain. We create appearances, then react to them.

You see again, *we are the creators.* And each creation is part of ourselves. This is the myth of Narcissus, who saw his image in the pool, fell in love with it and drowned in it, just as we do in our world full of our beloved forms, for which we fight and die.

I am not denying the reality of the cosmos. I am only denying that this sensory, three-dimensional level is all there is to perceive.

We are translating something, but in a limited way.

The point is this: Whatever you perceive on a given level—by level I mean a given state of cohesion—is perfectly valid on that level—*but on that level only*—as a reality. For example, a nightmare can be as painful as any waking event. However, what happens on one level of your being will not forcibly affect your totality. The car accident in your dream may wake you up screaming, but it won't break your bones. On the other hand, an atomic blast, if you are at its epicenter, would never be visually or otherwise perceived, and so would not affect your thoughts nor emotions because your body would be evaporated faster than the nerves could convey the message to the brain. You would be "disrobed" of your physical body without ever noticing it.

By now I imagine you have another question. "How can it be possible that I create my own world between my ears? We all see the same thing at once. A table, for instance."

Yes, we all have human eyes. And yes, the photons of light hit the energy field of the table. But none of us look from the same angle, and none of us see it in exactly the same way. So how is it done? Through a telepathic consensus emitted by our pineal gland. We emit our perception of something, and this creates the consensus. But each person brings a unique value to each perception. Take a great painting, for example. One person enters the museum especially to see it, and brings with her a knowledge, a love of that style of painting or the epoch it represents. Another may only see it as some meaningless daubs of paint. The guard who has to look at it every day will see it quite differently. So the telepathic consensus about that painting will have as many holes as a slice of Swiss cheese.

Consciousness

Let us now return to the common denominator, the field of energy. We need to discard our obsolete vision and look out at the world through new eyes. We ourselves, remember, are merely atoms. *We are fields of energy amid other fields of energy at different grades of cohesion.* Although the obsolete materialistic/mechanistic way of thinking considered the material world to be inanimate, it is in point of fact, consciousness. Everything is consciousness; there is no matter!

This is the oneness of which mystics speak. With this vision you will see a world of dynamics, a world of empowerment, where you and everything else are always fluid and changing, where reality is relative to the consciousness that perceives it, and where reality has countless dimensions.

We need to get in touch with the synthesis that is now taking place between the thousands of years of Eastern wisdom, and the last decades of mathematics of relativity and quantum physics in the West. They fit together wonderfully. This synthesis is the foundation, the basis of your new empowerment and of your new vision of the world, because you can apply it in a practical way to your own life.

The old mechanistic, divided vision of the world (separating "matter" from "spirit") created a constant feedback for all the tentative empowerments of a human being. Now, empowerment means receiving power. I don't mean being empowered by some law that permits you an activity—which is also a form of power. I mean this: receiving power to manifest yourself in a more ample way.

Most people are scared of power, and I believe rightly so: Because every time some power is manifested amid human beings, it's the use of the Big Stick principle. People get it on the head, and they'd rather not. They identify power with evil, with bad intentions, with someone taking advantage of someone else. A Mexican president once said, "What's the use of power, if you don't abuse it?" That seems a very typical human statement, don't you think?

What stops us from receiving empowerment? Well, everything that is in between the communication that is sending us that power and ourselves, our receiving consciousness. Mainly, superstition—belief in things that are not and never were—obsolete beliefs, conditioning, programming, moral hypocritical infrastructure. We take so many things for granted that our whole vision of the world is sustained, and our actions guided, by this concept of reality. It is sustained at an occult level by these infrastructures, many of which have come through our genes and chromosomes for thousands of years. And we believe that these infrastructures are the reality of our world manifestation.

The Answers to the Questions

Here, as I promised, are the answers to the two questions that my master posed many years ago. These are not like quick answers to a quiz. They are actually the result of many months of intense mental work by the students, and so constitute in themselves quite an effort to be understood. I will answer the second one first—the travel experience.

The German philosopher Immanuel Kant discovered that the human thinking machine could only conceive something as "real" if it had a cause, produced some effect, occupied some space, and had a duration. This necessity is built into our brains. So he called these categories "a-prioristic"—they are there before the thinking starts. Furthermore, our capacity of observation is limited to a rectangular frame, like a 70 mm movie screen—we do not have panoramic eyes like our house flies.

When I displace myself, say by walking, I can take in only one perceivable space at a time. As I move I perceive another, and so on, giving me the feeling of "change" in the scenery. As this happens in succession, it also gives me the feeling of time. Both feelings are overlaid and simultaneous.

But if I do all this from a helicopter, I will suddenly perceive many rectangular spaces of what was my previous scale of observation, all at one glance. All the "spaces" will be suddenly included into one vaster "space." If I am now in a space shuttle, all of the continent will become "my" space, and the previous spaces will become simultaneously *one*. If I should then look through binoculars at my previous starting point, the whole fragmented adventure will repeat itself because my field of vision will have again been reduced.

If you can now imagine yourself "out in space" beyond any star or perceivable bodies, without any point of reference, space will suddenly become a totally abstract concept with no reality to refer it to. Because by itself "space" never existed, but appears in our human experience as soon as our mind starts to focus and measure.

The essence in the story of the crash is much simpler.

We have already said that all and everything is but energy fields. As we contact them through our senses, we catalogue them as different "material" and give them a name in order to communicate between ourselves. This is our hardware.

Whatever is "happening" on our plane can always be reduced mentally to (1) its category—wood—cream—air; then (2) to its common denominator: energy. When seen through the senses these different densities interact; the most condensed breaking the more subtle, penetrating, dissolving, superimposing. Our flesh forms part of the circus, opposing itself to other elements, often being destroyed because it has a weak condensation compared to the many densities usually surrounding us.

The crash is therefore a play of energy oppositions, seen according to our limited senses as being "matter" that is hit, twisted, destroyed, or merely pushed. Awareness and emotional control in handling these "defined" fields of energy will avoid destructive oppositions, that is, crashes. Beyond our sensory limits, our consciousness, if only focused at the astral level, would not have noticed a thing. The crash, cops and all, took place as such only on this 3-D level. Let me remind you that unless our physical body is involved directly, what happens on other levels does not interact —each world, or dimension, having its own limits. The rapid frequencies of light which we call the high astral is one world; the extremely slow vibrations of the lithosphere, or low astral, is another.

Empowerment

So, when we speak of empowerment, we must consider the necessity of getting full control of the things that exist only in our mind. They are born from inner needs, inner thrusts provoked by fear, egoism, virtue, generosity—whatever. But they're all inside our consciousness; there's nothing "out there."

Now, the great "Laws of Nature" are the way we see Nature through our poor little five senses, which we organize in our mental card index, with our synapses and our circuits. We discover consequences, causes, final states, and beginnings with the usual mechanism of Reason, that most condensed part of our mind. Our built-in computer perceives, induces, deduces, and makes statements. And once the statement has been made, until the opposite of the deduction is proved it remains a law.

This is why a lot of our scientists state, *ex cathedra*, something about medicine, something about astronomy, something about the atom, whatever. But they always reserve themselves the right to say, "You know, science progresses, and what was black yesterday is now completely white." From that day on this white is very scientific, and there's no discussion about it—until somebody discovers it's "really" red, of course.

You see, we must be careful with the way we construct the world. Because the world is much more than so many colors and so many sounds, and the capacity of touching something that isn't too hot or isn't too cold or doesn't wiggle too much. There's much more than that.

So empowerment is to receive the power to amplify consciousness, and therefore, our world. You've heard the term "expansion of consciousness." Well, that's it. The expansion of consciousness is the path from Homo sapiens, through the next species, coming up to divinity. We are to become gods!

We cannot abandon all efforts, relax and lay back. We cannot become apes again. It was very easy going while it lasted, very comfortable, no problems, no taxes, no rent, nothing but a lot of fun. Big apes, you know, are not very easily attacked—they feel safe, and so they live happily in the jungle. But that's finished for us. We had the capacity all of a sudden to visualize something that we wanted and didn't have. And after that endless catastrophe began, because we always and endlessly want something else. So there you are. Forcibly, as we can't go down, we have to go up! This path that we are on, dear reader, is the path to divinity.

A lot of people will cry in horror: "This is terrible, sacrilegious. Blasphemy! It cannot be mentioned!"

Absurd. Why can it not be mentioned? Such exclamations are only the fruit of fear and ignorance. Such people are scared of the Boss.

I have been teaching for over forty-five years, and my students are intelligent. I am not dealing with the blissed-out spiritualist, or the person who can swallow anything as long as it has an oriental name. No, not at all. I have no turban on my head, nor a big flowing beard, and I don't look like a patriarch.

I deal with people who have their feet on the ground, though they may have their eyes on the stars. Look at the sequoia trees. They're tall as giants, their roots reach for miles. The wind cannot topple them, they won't budge. But the palm trees, they have big heads and very short roots, and when the tornado comes they fly off. And this for many spiritualists is the same thing.

My students have their heads firmly on their shoulders and have the capacity to obtain what they want from this plane. One of them (and many thereafter, through the years) asked me, "Why is it that you never speak of God?" I rarely mention God, because everybody puts into that symbol whatever values they have, so that doesn't help them very much in the beginning. But this fellow insisted: "Can you give us a definition, an idea, of what godhood is?"

Well, this has been a very controversial theme for centuries. Monks and friars, "shaven and shorn," desert hermits "all tattered and torn," bishops with bejewelled tiaras, and wise men well schooled in Greek and Latin, all beat their bald and hoary heads against what seemed impossible. But these theological geniuses found out a very good way to get out of the problem, to tiptoe out of it, as they generally do. They said, "You cannot define the Infinite." (Define: in Latin, *de finis* means "put a limit to.") They said, "How can you put a circle around something that has no limits? God has no limits. Therefore a rational definition is impossible. Forever, Amen!"

I took this for granted for quite a while, because it is a very logical explanation. Reason, as you have often heard by now, has its limitations, and trying to put Niagara Falls in a cup of tea just doesn't work. So, during one of my expansions into other dimensions, I had the joy of meeting a very advanced being and I told him, "Look, my students ask me something which puts me in a very uneasy position, because I cannot answer them. The question is how to define godhood. And as you over here well know, my profession as a traveler of the dimensions is to translate the incomprehensible into something clear and applicable." So he smiled and gave me a definition. Mind you well—only from that high level could such an incredible definition come down.

It will seem very simple. But I can promise you that if you know anything about meditation—that is, keeping quiet and focusing upon something in a definite and precise way—you can meditate upon these few words for the rest of your existence, and many more. And you still will not get to the bottom of it. The definition is clear: "God, or godhood, is the power to create *simultaneously* all the possible relations with everything in the cosmos."

Now everything in the cosmos means *everything*. That goes from a sheet of paper to the rings of Saturn to the animals on the bottom of the sea, and to every darn thing you can think of, material and immaterial. Thoughts, concepts, feelings, hopes, desires, fears, loves, hatreds, *everything in the cosmos*. Relate to all of it, all the details of it, the myriads of myriads, and all this *simultaneously*: That means instantaneously, all at the same time. If you can do that, you have no more problems—you're God.

That's it. Now, that's a powerful definition. It doesn't limit divinity, it makes its expansion comprehensible. Go and tell that to the poor shepherds in Galilee two thousand years ago, it couldn't work. But as today you can understand what inner silence is, what inner traveling is, I can give you this formula, this aphorism. Sit and meditate upon this incredible statement. It will make you infinitely empowered. As you follow along the details and the branching out, you will rise from one level of comprehension to another and another!

Many authors have become rich writing books on helping people to acquire more energy, that is money (which is a form of energy), and who advise you to "Think Rich." I tell you: "Think Divine."

It's more riches, that's all.

HEARING THE VOICE OF SILENCE

Our freedom is so much greater than we have comprehended. We can learn to shift from reality to reality.

LAWRENCE LESHAN

My understanding of the fundamental laws of the universe did not come out of my rational mind.

ALBERT EINSTEIN

If we are willing to examine the agitation of our own mind and look just beyond it, we quite readily find entry into rooms that hold surprising possibilities: a greater inner calm, sharper concentration, deeper intuitive understanding . . .

RAM DASS/PAUL GORMAN

All the resources of our almost miraculous technology have been thrown into the current assault against silence.

ALDOUS HUXLEY

Stop talking, stop thinking, and there is nothing you will not understand.

SENG TS'AN

Chapter 5

HEARING THE VOICE OF SILENCE

In this book we are constantly speaking of levels, and before we can accept that the voice of Silence comes to us from a higher level, we need to comprehend their existence. Even theoretical science now speaks of different dimensions. We are all trying to express the multidimensional nature of reality.

Multidimensional Reality

Please imagine a sheet of ordinary white paper. This will be the symbol of our three-dimensional plane. Now imagine a neat little hole in the paper, through which a small ball comes and goes at such an incredible speed that we cannot perceive the moments of its absence (like a rotating fan, which seems to be a blurry disc). Therefore the ball, even though it is not always there, is ever present to our senses.

Now imagine a great number of these balls, like the dots that form a newspaper photo or a TV image. Grouped together in darks and lights, they allow us to see people and landscapes on *this* side of our sheet of paper, in our world. But the opposite hemispheres of the balls compose a different picture, the only one seen by anyone on the other side of the paper, a picture seemingly just as permanent, but quite another one.

Next imagine this ball, because of its incredible speed, also going up and down, crosswise to the first path; then at 45 degrees; then less; and so on and so on. It would then present its faces—again because of its speed—*simultaneously* in many directions, forming infinite realities at the same time. This is what happens to the subatomic particles studied by quantum physicists. The particles and waves are unpredictable; they defy the principle of causality *because they manifest themselves as multidimensional simultaneity.* They do not follow our linear, causal vision at all—in fact, they disappear from it!

Now imagine this little ball forming a segment, the rotating segment forming a disc, the disc a column, another column forming surfaces, and a reality has appeared. But just take away the little ball and twenty worlds have vanished.

Or did they?

Of course not. They have never existed, they just appeared to be. This brings us to a major postulate: A *reality is defined by the limitations of the consciousness that perceives it.*

This needs a little explaining. A consciousness—that is, an entity, an individual—is aware of what it perceives. Fine. But according to its capacity of perception (through however many senses it may have) it can perceive so much and no more. This will be its reality, composed of what it can perceive *and* elaborate of these perceptions. A person born deaf and blind lives one reality; but is it yours? Evidently not, if you have your five senses. Now, on whatever level this may be, the mechanics and results will be the same. "Expansion of consciousness" simply means adding the means to perceive more, elaborating more, until the relations of this consciousness with the cosmos would be total—and this would be enlightenment.

Each perceived reality will have its own limits. And each reality—call it level or dimension, if you like—will be real as long as you do not jump into another, the impact of which jump would make the last one seem a dream.

Intuition

I teach my students to become travelers of the dimensions. But nobody actually travels, nobody "goes" anywhere. Rather, they "tune in." Each individual is like a little radio set, which can only tune in certain wavelengths, certain frequencies, as an inexpensive radio can only tune clearly the local stations. With expansion of consciousness—empowerment—the same radio can pick up more and more waves, short, long, ultra-high-speed waves.

Now let us try to tune in to the voice of silence. This is Intuition. It is superior to Reason because it comes from a higher frequency level than this rational one.

First of all, the *sine qua non* condition of Intuition is perception. I think you will agree that what is unperceived might as well not be. And at the high-decibel level in which we live, we are deafened. In this age, to try to hear Intuition, the voice of silence, is like trying to hear and enjoy the delicate sounds of a flute or a violin in a discotheque blaring out hard rock. We won't hear anything.

Outer noise and inner noise. We are deafened by the shouts of Reason and Emotions, who are always fighting each other like mother-in-law and daughter-in-law. They are constantly fighting because Reason is the policeman of our life. It was brought up, created, polished, and sent to work to stop us doing irrational things. And on this three-dimensional level it is often quite a help.

So how do we get hold of Intuition? How do we perceive and receive it? Intuitive thought is never based upon concatenation—chains of thinking—and linkage of rational data, such as developed and explainable facts. It comes from the world of everywhere, all-the-time, now. That is the world that *is*. Therefore it appears to us as something complete, something that is already accomplished.

Intuition always takes us by surprise. It gives us a feeling Reason doesn't.

Here is what happens. We need to apply the valuable information of Intuition to our practical life, so we bring it down to the rational level. Because we feel we must find a way to express the intuitive idea here, where we live. But "here" is not everywhere, all the time, now. "Here" is the three-dimensional world with its categories of time/space/cause and effect. Therefore, when we have to decide a certain course of action, when we must define the time and place, Reason takes over. Intuition brings messages Reason has no images for, so therefore it will attack them.

Reason is an analytical machine (analysis in Greek means dissolution). As soon as this machine gets hold of our intuitive plan, which is complete in itself, it goes up in arms. "What is this? Where does this come from? Where is the cause that generated this idea? I need a cause or I won't let anything happen. I will sabotage anything that comes from that source. I hate mysteries. I only accept clear facts!"

Then our Emotions, which have of course arisen at the moment of the intuition, say, "This is wonderful, I feel great! I feel like the King of Kings. I will act."

And Reason snaps back, "You will not act, you fool. You don't know where this comes from. Therefore it is dangerous. It is not rational. I won't let it pass."

The energy spent in that sort of confusion is absolutely incredible. This is why we're constantly hesitating. We rarely know, with absolute certainty, what we should do.

This makes such a fuss, it makes such a lot of noise, it is so scandalously loud that the voice of silence becomes totally lost. Probably when we're through the hassle of discussing, the offer of Intuition is not even valid any more.

So what do we do? What is the next step?

Silence.

Silence

Let's see how we can handle intuition, daily life, and silence.

We have to find a way to perceive the intuitive thought in its totality. It never seems complex, because it does not have the explanatory system and mechanics. It just appears to us *as is*. Now, how can we hold this presence, this voice, which only in silence is perceivable? We must use the correct techniques.

This is one of the great differences between religious orientations and Esoteric orientations. Both give you the same advice, the same morality, the same laws, a dramatic simplification of great truths. But the religions give no techniques! They tell you, "You must not do this"—but they don't tell you how are you going to handle your desires and passions. Whereas the Esoteric line does. Esoteric refers to teaching which is hidden, given out only to a few, those who are prepared.

Projecting Reverence

This technique is extremely simple. But it takes practice to be effective: Create an atmosphere of peace and silence and enter a state of reverence. If you are in the state of reverence, Reason will be left behind. Wait for images to come in. When they do, project reverence on them. When reverence is projected on anything, its essence appears. The images that come in reverence are from beyond the rational. Whatever appears, feel it. Don't explain. Soon you will have useful intuitions.

When you project reverence through your attention on anyone or anything, you will experience four effects. First, you will perceive the immediate vision of the subject in simplicity—all adornments dissolve. The inner values of a human will appear in transparency. Next, you will feel this as a final, naked truth, your inner truth about the subject. Third, your action or evaluation will be done in purity, as it never is mingled with thoughts or passions. Finally, you will receive a superhuman vision of the subject observed, the vision through the third eye, the "vision of the Initiate."

Silence Through the Hot Line

If you are just beginning the practice of meditation, you will be distracted by the inner noise. How do we obtain total silence? Through the *hot line*—a permanent and constant relation with the level, or world, or vibrations, where the intuitive elements *are constantly present*. We do not receive an intuition as we receive a postcard. First you must use techniques to silence the monkey cage of constantly fighting emotions. You leave them as you would leave the train whistles when you are on a plane—you go so far that you don't hear them anymore. The trains go on whistling, but you don't hear them anymore, you're somewhere else.

This "somewhere else" is the permanent level of everywhere, all-the-time, and is constantly present. It is the level of *now*. It is as though we lived always under the clouds. Periodically and unpredictably we perceive some part of the blue sky when the clouds part a little. Otherwise, we are constantly under the cloud-laden sky. But, in fact, the blue is always there.

So when we can, through silence, lift ourselves to this above-cloud level, we get the total picture of the One That Is.

You will ask, "Then why in the world must I suffer so much under the clouds when I have this possibility of blue sky?"

Well, all do not have this possibility. That is a state of grace—to use the theological definition. If you can remain in a state of grace—that is, union or syntony with high frequencies—you will have no problem.

Fortunately, theology—which means "knowledge of divinity" (and is in fact only the sum of opinions of people with a belief-system), does not monopolize the state of grace. This state of consciousness can often be experienced through the reverence that comes down from the starlit sky with its awe-inspiring sense of eternity. It is the undisturbed relation of the soul with its own essence, felt simultaneously as the roots of our becoming and as the direct way of our return Home.

Simultaneity? Everywhere, all-the-time, now? Rationally, it's absolute insanity. Reason cannot conceive it. Because of its mechanics, Reason has no way of understanding that something that "has been," is "present," and that what is present is at the same time the future. Reason will say, "Come on, how does this work? I mean, after all, I eat three times a day, three-hundred-and-sixty-five times a year—are you telling me that I've eaten all these meals in one shot?"

That's laughable, isn't it? And it can hardly be explained on the rational level. Why? Because Reason, although it goes through all our daily experiences, and witnesses our living "simultaneously," cannot conceive it as such because of its mechanics, and must extend and develop this simultaneity through "time."

For instance, when I drive a car on the freeway I must be very attentive to the signs and all the other drivers around me. At the same time I am eating a candy and tasting it. I am also listening to very pleasant music, smelling the ocean air, holding my girl's hand, and discussing with her the rational facts about the furniture we shall put in the new apartment. All this I do *simultaneously* in the fraction of a second. We've all done it, more or less in the same fashion.

Can reason conceive it? No.

But we *experience* it. When I try to explain it to you, I have to produce a series of frames, like a moving picture, each change being another frame.

So that is what creates time: the successive changes in *duration*, each changing segment with its own quality. When duration (this sensation of ours) undergoes no modification, then we lose the concept of time.

Conceiving, for Reason, means thinking in images. And the images must be thought in *succession*. It just cannot put in one and the same frame anything with the slightest change. You can have the building of the pyramids and thirty thousand slaves—but if one of them moves an eyelash, it's another picture, another frame.

So Reason is an instrument that stands totally apart from our experience. We experience immediately, instantaneously, many different levels of perception that Reason cannot conceive because of its mechanics.

This is why, when we explain the inexplicable, we have to produce *symbols*. For instance, the four-sided pyramid in Teotihuacán, near Mexico City, is a very interesting example. It is a symbol of time and simultaneity. If you walk along the base of the pyramid, on the physical ground, you don't see the other sides—that is your future, it is not visible for you. And the sides you have passed are only in your memory, they are not present, you don't perceive them anymore.

If you climb, with effort, to the first grade, then you still will do the same thing. Symbolically this level represents the astral world, or molecular level, more rapid, more subtle. But the phenomenon will be identical. However, you cover much more rapidly (because you are part of the pyramid now) the surface that the pyramid covers at the base. Then you make another effort, you go to the second level (which represents the mental level), and you find yourself with the same phenomenon, but much more rapidly.

And when you finally sit up in the Teocali, which is translated as "the house of the gods," you sit at the sum of the pyramid. You cover all the pyramid because you are part of it. You cover the same terrain without movement, the past, present, and future. You are the sum of it all. So, you see, this symbol was comprehensible if you had the capacity to grasp it. But rationally speaking, it had to become a whole long story, because Reason cannot conceive simultaneity.

So, this level that we must reach, this Intuition, is a *state of being*. It is not the distribution of little bits of goodies here and there during the life of a human, it is a state of being. And as we cannot simultaneously be in all the levels, including the rational one, which is the one that puts the bricks together when we have to build something, we must create the hot line. And that's done through meditation, contemplation, and hard work—then we are constantly in contact with the intuitive level. We do not get a little patch of blue, we get the whole sky.

The intuitive level is a state of grace. And in that state of grace you have absolutely no problems, because they're solved before they were even started.

So this is what Intuition is. This is part of silence. And it is also part of a new lifestyle. If we go on living the good old way, we shall suffer as usual—because of the inevitable unpredictability. We never know what's happening the next second. Any minute we might have an earthquake. Mr. Richter of the Richter Scale signed no contract with the elemental forces of Earth. We might have any magnitude of tremor—it isn't said that it must be 7 or 8. Why not 28? We don't know. We never know.

So you must connect to the intuitive level by the hot line. Then at any moment, if you place yourself in the right state of consciousness, you receive the news, the information, *as you need it*. This is the fruit of inner silence. And this is why this book has its reason to be: Through it (didn't I say it was a door?) you will gain the empowerment without which there is no quantum leap.

The Steps to Correct Meditation

Now here, as I promised you earlier, are the steps to correct meditation, leading to contemplation.

First you must dissolve the sensation of having a physical body, and the emotions must be frozen (see page 22). Now you practice concentration.

Concentrate on an object or an abstraction—a symbol like a triangle, or a sentence like the definition of godhood I gave you earlier (see page 48). Concentration is bringing all the light of our mental capacity to focus on the vision of the details of the chosen object or sentence. It must be, as in a show window, perfectly clear. When you obtain this clarity, pass to the next step, meditation.

In meditation you take that object or symbol or sentence, turning it around, move it upside down, right to left, left to right—handling it as you would handle an antique art object, to see every detail of it.

Then you *enter* the object of your meditation. Think of its age, its dynamics, its value, what it is as a symbol. If it is a sentence, think of all its meanings, and of every word contained in it. This branches out into dozens and dozens of channels which you follow up, *always coming back to the base.* When you are through, when there is nothing left to know about it—when all the details, and relations, and extrapolations are exhausted and there is nothing left in the crucible—you may pass into contemplation. The contemplation of that same object, thought, or sentence will be the cognition of it in other dimensions of its existence.

Let's take an example. Concentrate on a diamond. You see the diamond with all its facets. You can see it perfectly, shining, refracting light, a crystal prism. You see it from left, right, behind, above. After looking at it in precise vision, you pass on to meditation. Here you enter into its value, both earthly and Esoteric. What is a diamond? Humans put very high value on it. A diamond is a concentrated field of energy that has been pressurized from coal, the mineral which it was, into a translucent prism. In that prism we have the possibility to subdivide the light of the sun, which represents life and therefore cosmic love. When it has been cut, the diamond will send out rays of light, therefore giving out in its own fashion light and love. Seen from the Esoteric viewpoint, this diamond is a precious object—a translation of the "giver of life," the sun, like the crystal that it is. So this is the meditation on the diamond: What are its possibilities? What does it do? What are its wonderful qualities? When all this is exhausted, and there is no more to be achieved, you enter with that diamond into contemplation.

There the process of thought is abandoned. The vision of the diamond still appears, then vanishes, and you enter yourself into the great chimney of light that has been created at the end of meditation, from where all intuitive information is received. You feel your consciousness, your awareness, rise to the upper part of your head. You enter into contemplation at the crown *chakra* at the top of your head. Here you receive no information, no thoughts, no details. You slowly *become* the object itself. You are the diamond. Through you light shines, and you emit light. You receive light from many angles, you have become the object you concentrated and meditated upon.

Now unity has been achieved and all characteristics will jell in your consciousness, as you have become the diamond. In this way you can become a blade of grass, or a flower, or anything—anything being virtually nothing, a field of energy.

When you blend into any field of energy through contemplation you become covibrant with that vibration and tonality. At that level there is no duality.

This is correct meditation. As you progress, try it with objects, then symbols, and then abstractions, such as Beauty or Truth. Or try a sentence: "I Am Love Manifesting"; "I Am The One That Is." When you are advanced in the work, meditate on simultaneity. Not only will it give you gooseflesh, it will create new brain circuits.

Retraction of the Senses

The monks of Tibet, wanting nothing more in this life than to attain liberation from the human condition, used to have themselves walled up for long periods of time, often for years. This method of getting away from it all provided absolute silence. No communications from the outside world—no novelties, no information, no distractions. Though this method appears somewhat drastic to us today, it cannot be denied that we are just as drastically assaulted by noise and lack of privacy. Surely we need peace and silence more than any society in the history of this planet. Here, then, is the Tibetan technique for retraction of the senses, without the need for a walled-up cave.

Find a quiet place where you will not be disturbed or interrupted. Unplug the telephone, if that is possible. Make sure the temperature of the room is the way you like it, and that your clothing is loose and comfortable. Sit in a posture of meditation. Relax. Take several slow, deep breaths. Take away the energy of the physical body (see page 21), then freeze the astral body of emotions (see page 22). Don't hurry the process.

Now take away the clothing on your body, by *visualizing* its disappearance. Do this just as you took away the energy from the physical body, from the feet up to the crown of the head. Begin with the toes. See the socks or stockings melt away; then the trouser legs or skirt; the belt vanishes; the shirt, inch by inch, the shirt-sleeves, the collar is slowly gone. Do this until there is nothing left. All has melted away. You are naked.

Let your hands rest easily on your lap, in whatever position is most natural. But—and this is important—the hands should not be in a *mudra* or gesture of meditation. They should be open. You will thus lose the sense of touch.

Now raise the energy up to the *Ajna chakra*. This is located in the forehead, between the brows, the site of the third eye. Just keep your awareness there. Don't try to visualize any images. Don't follow any thoughts. Your awareness stays between the eyebrows.

Swallow once. That's it. There will be no more saliva accumulating so that you are conscious of having to swallow.

Now listen to the sound of the blood in your ears—the heartbeat pulsing. You hear only this noise. No other sound. It fills your ears.

Breathe very shallowly and very slowly, about twelve to fourteen breaths a minute.

Keep the awareness between the eyebrows. You may hear background noises—your neighbor turns on a radio, a gardener starts up a power mower—but simply dismiss them. Give them no value. Use these noises to realize your separation from them. They are of the world; you have withdrawn from the world.

You may see some pictures on your mindscreen. Ignore them. You are not interested, just resting gently in a state of complete serenity. You are pure awareness. You have found inner silence, and the rest will slowly evaporate and fade away.

If you like, after you have practiced this retraction of the senses meditation several times, you may add a few further steps.

Once you have reached serenity and silence, imagine that you are on a mountain, and that overhead is a night sky filled with stars. A vast black expanse covered with brilliant, glittering stars. Though you remain with eyes closed and do not look up, the presence of the beautiful sky fills you with a deep sense of reverence.

This reverence then expresses itself in compassion for everything that lives. From your heart send compassion out to all beings in all worlds.

Above the crown of your head is dazzling white light.

Visualize your body as completely dissolved.

Rest in the state of pure, serene, loving awareness.

CREATING AWARENESS

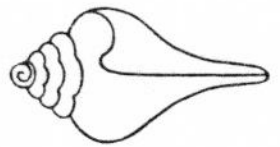

Mindfulness is the miracle by which we master and restore ourselves . . . it can call back in a flash our dispersed mind and restore it to wholeness so that we can live each minute of life.

THICH NHAT HANH

Come, look at this world, glittering like a royal chariot; the foolish are immersed in it, but the wise are not attached to it.

TEACHINGS OF THE BUDDHA

Meditation means awareness; to be aware of what you are doing, what you are thinking, what you are feeling, aware without any choice, to observe, to learn.

KRISHNAMURTI

Curb your tongue and senses
And you are beyond trouble.
Let them loose
And you are beyond help.

LAO TZU

Under all speech that is good for anything there lies a silence that is better. Silence is deep as Eternity; speech is shallow as Time.

THOMAS CARLYLE

Chapter 6

CREATING AWARENESS

Awareness is the greatest treasure we have. If a man who is anxious about his business and a woman who is full of fear should go to the beach at night, would either one be aware of the serene beauty of moonlight on the ocean? The moon and ocean might as well not be there. Consciousness only illuminates what it is aware of.

Imagine an immense field at night, littered with objects. A spotlight moves over it—the spotlight is the consciousness that brings into awareness whatever it lights up. As this spot of "reality" moves over the dark field, the rest recedes into oblivion. Of course, this is just a simile—but let's take it a step further. If the spotlight is put out, there's nothing there. If the sun rises, there's everything!

We receive many, many stimuli from the cosmos. Some we translate; most we cannot. We use the ones we translate to create the shapes around us—people and things—and put value to them.

Other people define us in the same way. They create their own world and they confirm *our own* presence in *our own* world by objectivizing us, by creating us with their senses. If nobody else could perceive us, we would feel like ghosts!

We believe we have an objective world because others translate the stimuli in the same way we do. This is because their construction is identical to ours. (By construction I mean the condensation of vibrations at the atomic level, translated by our senses.)

We translate the stimuli through nerve terminals that project on an inner mindscreen. If we can create other areas of subtle perception, through specific effort and work, we shall be able to translate more and thereby increase our awareness. We shall have a much stronger spotlight that throws light on a much wider field, illuminates more of the cosmos, and therefore relates to more of the cosmos. Remember the definition of godhood?

Three Dimensions of Being

Let me return for a moment to our three vehicles. We have a trinity of bodies, or energy levels: physical, astral, and mental. This trinity might also be called cellular, molecular, and electronic; or physical, emotional, intellectual.

Every condensed atomic structure which we call a cell is in motion and active because it has an *astral* body and aura around and inside it. By astral I mean more subtle. An astral body automatically exists in conformity to the *physical* body. The physical body is really just a more condensed energy: It condensed from the astral prenatal blueprint. So, we have a three-dimensional physical model of the astral, in addition, we have an even more subtle—but still identical—*mental* construction.

The electronic current of the mental body is similar to the other two bodies in the same way that our circulatory system is like a sort of internal blood suit—identical to the physical, going from the top of the head to the nerves of the toes. There is really nothing mysterious about an astral conformity to the physical, and an electronic conformity that pushes and moves the astral. The electronic or mental body creates the *images* that make the astral fluctuate and move, and finally moves the autonomic nervous system.

Each of the bodies has a different receiving and communication system, different terminals, different sensitivities. Each of them receives stimuli from "above" or "around." Normally, we are not aware of these stimuli, because we only translate the messages from our five senses.

Although the trinity interacts as a unity, we need to extend, stretch, become intensely aware of the trinity. All three are of different densities, of different worlds; and they receive, command, and act through different phenomenology. Becoming aware of the three systems will lead to *evidences* that different worlds exist, parallel worlds—other dimensions of reality.

Your five senses put you in contact with what we call the physical world—they permit you to see the mountains, the stars, to hear the sounds of a bird or a cannon. In the same way, your astral body is part of a world that is an extension of—not identical to—the physical. The mental body commands a world of electronic extension that is unlimited, far beyond the speed of light.

Try this exercise: Feel yourself. In silence, be aware of yourself. Try to extend when the physical terminal nerves are quiet and the physical brain is about to sleep, to rest after the day's work. Or feel out, through daydream, into the astral levels. Explore the sensitivity of the other bodies which are your property. They are more than that: You live in and through them in different dimensions.

Let the spotlight of your consciousness play on the different dimensions of your being. The beginning of full awareness is expansion, understanding the possibility of expanded consciousness, reasoning out its mechanics, and dwelling on it until it becomes second nature.

Automatisms

Awareness is the key to freedom from the limitations of human existence. I would like you to think about this for a moment. Like all the steps to empowerment, it is simple—but it is far from easy.

The problem is that we dream our lives away, always planning, always projecting for the next moment, or hour, or even years ahead. Planning isn't wrong; but we put so much emotion into imagining results, positive or negative, that we drain ourselves dry. We plan and we prepare, and we haven't got the least idea what's going to happen. In almost every instance the event we have been worrying so much about never comes to pass. Life in the physical and in the astral is completely unpredictable. When we are worried, we are without awareness—and one cannot walk in the path of power and wisdom in a noisy cloud of preoccupation.

This has been a recurring theme in all the literature that deals with the process of inner development. As the Chinese say, awareness is difficult because we are constantly "fascinated by the ten thousand things of this world." Therefore our consciousness is totally dispersed, drawn out and away from the central axis. The insistence on the need for awareness runs like a golden vein through the work of many authors: Gustav Meyerink said this in his book *The Golem*, and G. I. Gurdjieff taught generations of seekers: "Remember yourself." The scriptures also advised the power of self-presence: "Watch therefore, for ye know neither the day nor the hour wherein the Son of man cometh" (Matthew 24:42); "Behold, I come as a thief. Blessed is he that watcheth" (Revelation 14:15).

But some technical details have never been given, and this is the reason for deep confusion. It took me years to realize the difference between being aware of the overall daily activity, and the incredible quantity of *conditioned automatisms* built up over centuries, which handle the habitual acts through which we function daily—shaving, picking up spoons and forks, dressing, even driving. But since they are assimilated in our three vehicles, they constitute our human capital. We must never analyze them or take them apart as one would a toy or a clock. They are past experiences, tested, accepted, and sent back to our computer to be ready to reappear as they are, with rare additions or changes. Some were formed during childhood, some later, but all constitute the pattern of a given culture.

The attempt to become aware of their details would require a dissolution: Each automatic action is composed of years of concentrated effort. It is good to be aware that we are using them, but not to dissolve each one into its constitutive elements. After all, you don't take your wristwatch apart and put it together again whenever you want to know the time. With the spotlight of awareness and techniques, it is possible to rid yourself of negative automatisms or bad habits. See page 115, chapter 9.

Continuity of Awareness

We need not only to increase our capacity for awareness, but to develop a *continuity*. We remember our past only in isolated peaks. We feel there is no continuity to our dreams because of the periods of oblivion between them. The same thing happens thousands of times during the day—little blackouts, when the consciousness is focused elsewhere. And there are the longer blackouts of sleep and death.

The importance of continuity of awareness just can't be overestimated—it goes far beyond our ordinary daily affairs to the cycles of death and rebirth: It relates to the great world theories about reincarnation. The last time I heard the late Krishnamurti speak, someone asked him his opinion on the subject. He seemed to hesitate a moment, and then said, "Oh yes, reincarnation—it is an idea that gives my people a lot of consolation."

There is another story, also involving a celebrity, although of a different type— Dr. D. T. Suzuki, the Japanese Zen master, was once invited by the famous psychologist Eric Fromm to give a series of conferences at the University of Mexico. As he was walking to the conference, I asked him, "Doctor, what is your opinion on reincarnation?"

He stopped in his tracks and said, "Reincarnation is a fact. But of course it doesn't exist."

I was left with my head swirling. It took me years to digest this answer, especially since it came from an authority of the world's most serious school of spirituality.

So how do awareness and eventual reincarnation get tied together?

Awareness is an axis around which all our functions revolve, *with whatever vehicle we are then identified.* Do you realize the implications?

The statement made by Dr. Suzuki haunted me for years. If reincarnation, as he said, didn't exist, then really, the whole of manifestation was a farce! With no continuity, no consequences, the saint and the crook would both be right! Why make any effort at all?

The first understanding I received was that Dr. Suzuki meant "no awareness, no memory of oneself, no reincarnation." And, as the majority of humans dream their lives, they create no center of constant referral to a continuity. It is then not reincarnation, but a recycling of anonymous, amnesic elements. The physical brain, which has been put together to store memory, will disintegrate at death. The whole package goes. When the elements that compose us return to manifestation — attracted by affinity toward future parents — without awareness everything is lost. A new brain is given. We are recycled, as is everything else. Thus the question so many ask, with so much anguish — "Will I return?" — is easily answered.

"Of course, everything returns. Only as you will not be aware of it, it might as well be somebody else."

That is why you must create awareness *here and now*.

"Return" is not what we hope is meant by "reincarnation." Not by a long shot. Some tendencies may be brought to our consciousness once in a while, such as attractions or fears or phobias. But when a person says, "I was so and so at a given place and time," he or she is only speaking of fractions of a life, like one minute out of a three-hour film — no continuity, no reference to an end or beginning. The new blank brain we are given by Mama has no mnemonic circuits from God knows whom, when, and where! There have been rare cases of recall in children whose rational power was still in formation. Something had impressed their emotional memory; and through some association of thoughts, in this life the past impression was evoked, producing images of people and places.

But a developed awareness extends itself to subtle frequencies. When practiced *here and now*, it transfers itself — to the astral and mental levels, establishing a beachhead of a permanent "I am" in both of them. This is what we can hang onto and recognize as an axis of continuity. It is but a thread, and seems very fragile, but it is quite permanent. It is of infinite value to the serious seeker, allowing him or her to subsist until the final stages are reached, and multiplicity transmutes into the One.

Awareness, this axis of energy, is like a giant twister, sustaining in its dynamics every element of our manifestation. And like the twister, when its energy has been reabsorbed, leaves at its base nothing but unrelated, meaningless rubbish. It is through the dominion of awareness that we shall understand the mystery of consciousness and hold in the permanent silence which reigns in the eye of the storm the magic wand of empowerment at all our conscious levels of existence.

Exercises for Awareness

I hope I have convinced you by this point of the enormous need of awareness. The rest of this chapter will list for you some tricks of the trade. Here are practical exercises and techniques you can begin to use right away.

A Beachhead for the Astral

This first exercise develops the power to send out beyond the death barrier an actual message to yourself beyond death. To do this you must be a spectator of your own life. Remind yourself by making little signs that say "I AM AWARE" and put them everywhere—on your bathroom mirror, your car dashboard, the door of your refrigerator. Make as many as you can.

These reminders will not only augment your awareness during the day, they will carry over into the dream state. Their constant presence will sink the message into your subconscious, just as most of our daily props reappear in the dream world. Your dreams will become more vivid. And if you become aware during a dream, you are master of the situation—you have achieved a leap toward liberation. You have, if you do it faithfully, practically achieved mastery over an infinity of dimensions.

Creating Continuity of Awareness

Another way to help continuity of awareness is to create your own jingle. Make it very catchy, like a commercial you can't forget even if you want to. Make it an affirmation: "I am observing myself at every moment, I am aware, here and now, here and now, living in the present moment . . ." Use your own words. Set it to music. It's even better if you can get it to rhyme. Let it sing in your mind constantly for a week.

This will create a new imprint, changing forever the way you act, sit, and talk. Before the jingle you did these things in a dispersed, unaware fashion. Sing the jingle for two months and you will acquire a centering that is priceless. You will look people straight in the eye. Your unity of three bodies will do exactly what you want it to do.

Once this has been accomplished, you may want to get rid of the jingle—you will probably be more than tired of it. The way to do this is to replace it with another jingle, one that you do not find so catchy. (Some students of mine used "The Bunny Hop.") This replacement will then be easy to drop.

Being Mindful of Water

Another technique for awareness is to be mindful of water. Our bodies are more than 80 percent water. It is an element we are very closely related to—it's good to have an affinity with it. Every time you take a drink of water, be aware of its qualities, and remember that without it you would not survive. Try to remember to be grateful for the gift of "Sister Water," as St. Francis called it. Every time you bathe, or wash your hands, address Sister Water with reverence and silently say, "Thank you, Sister Water, for your power, your purity, and your patience." Water is a vehicle for elements of all kind, but in its essence is always pure. This exercise provides the opportunity to bring your awareness home several times a day.

Becoming Aware of the Power of Thoughts

We need to become aware of the power of our thoughts. We are conditioned to think that only what goes through our five senses is real. But on higher levels, thoughts are realities—*they are real.* If they were not, artistic creations or inventions would never jell into what we call matter. Our thoughts create forms on other levels, and these "thought forms" affect us and others. As we rid our mind of obsolete superstitions it becomes clearer, our thoughts become sharper, and our responsibility for them becomes greater.

When we construct a clear castle of thoughts, there is an emission astrally and mentally. Through the pores of the skin a signal is emitted. This emission hits the field of energy outside of us and starts modifying that field. For instance, fear is a thought form with an emotion attached which hits the glandular system. A dog can smell fear astrally. So can a horse, even a tarantula. We emit thoughts just as we emit brain waves, heat, odors. Therefore we are responsible for them.

We must stop manifesting negative thoughts. These loaded images, loaded with intentions, explode into many dimensions. These emissions constitute a layer of astrality around us. A negative thought is surely alive, even though it is not visible—an image is as ready to go as a bullet. Hurting someone you love with words is just like hitting them physically. Anger comes by being involved in an action through your own limitation. You are too fascinated with your world, too hung up on it.

But, you ask, how can we stop being negative? Be aware of your limitations. This will help avoid frustration, the source of most anger.

Becoming Aware of the Pleasure/Pain Syndrome

It is extremely helpful to train yourself to become aware of the pleasure/pain syndrome. We seek pleasure, but we also seek to avoid its other face, pain. Pain comes with pleasure, whether we like it or not. They are inseparable. For example, if you have the pleasure of falling in love, you have without any doubt acquired also the pain of separation from that person. If you have the pleasure of eating the double-fudge sundae, you have the pain of dieting to compensate, or of your poor Brother Donkey dealing with all that sugar.

Be aware of the *mechanics* of seeking pleasure, be aware that it creates differences from others. It creates ego satisfaction, and this can lead to the arousal of negative emotions. If a new, show-off millionaire drives his Rolls Royce through skid row, he will attract much negative emotion.

The Power of Nonidentification

Awareness is also the power of *nonidentification.* Stand aside to look dispassionately at your emotional storms, financial needs, career obstacles. Yes, there are emotions and there are problems, but being caught up in them creates clouds. Our problems come from our stubborn identification with this condensed level. It's the suffering that makes this reality seem so real. Because you live in the physical machine, you will suffer; however, with awareness you will see all the ramifications of an action before you do it.

Be concentrated, involved, and effective, yet never identify yourself with a lower vibration unless you want to fall to that level. Love with all your heart, give it all away if you wish to, but never identify yourself. On the contrary: Lift to your level, through daily care and responsibility, the object of your love; then your love will be constructive beyond life. You can't lift a drowning person out of the water in mid-ocean if you are in the same condition. But you can if you have a raft.

Always obtain your joys without hurting others. Enjoy whatever you want, as long as it hurts no one—including yourself. Avoid doing anything that belittles you or diminishes you in any way. Enjoy your pleasures, avoid pain—that's fine, as long as it's with awareness. And remember that the awareness of a joy makes it stronger.

Observing Yourself from a Higher Level

If you can observe yourself from a *higher level,* you won't create clouds of identification. It is always a mistake to try to solve a problem on the level where the problem occurs. Go up and look down on it. Once you have stopped identifying with it, you can see it more clearly.

On this level we have many obstacles. From a higher level we can dissolve them. Always make decisions in a high state of consciousness.

Try this exercise: From a sublime, high level, look down at yourself. You will have a different vision. Watch yourself as you do things with emotion, make projections into the future, have expectations. It's like removing the roof of your house and seeing everything you do inside. From a high level or vibration, you will hardly recognize yourself at a low vibration. You may be ashamed of what you're doing, but you cannot hide from yourself. In some religious disciplines, this is called "practicing the presence of God."

Becoming Nonjudgmental

It is very beneficial to lose the habit of being judgmental. Judgment comes from the ego. To be able to look at other beings without judgment means that the obstacle of the ego has been dissolved.

As you see a woman pass by you can with one glance evaluate the price, the stylishness, the good taste of her clothes. In so doing you bring to bear on your judgment all the fruit of your education, culture, or professional experience—and you do this a thousand times a day. And for free! This is the result of our ego, which constantly, by evaluating the possessions of others, situates itself socially. When it feels itself in an inferior position, the ego sends Reason out in search of excuses for its lack of power and possessions: "Yes, I have no Rolls Royce, but I am handsome and young and he isn't!"

Judgment means evaluation. We lose a lot of valuable energy when we try to evaluate everything we see. This is why going shopping is so tiring—you judge every single thing you see and give it a value, which is a big energy drain. And energy, my friends, is power. We must not throw away energy at any level, we must save it.

Here is a Taoist technique to create and use energy: Stand straight and extend your hands and fingertips, palms down. Keep your hands together, as though very delicate cobwebs joined your slightly parted fingertips. Keep your eyes on your hands as you move them steadily and slowly from right to left, then left to right, five times. Then bring your hands in front of you and cup them to feel the ball of energy which your hands have created. Take that ball and put it wherever you wish—head, throat, groin, stomach, heart—wherever energy is most needed at the time.

Awareness of Silence

In your daily life, be meditative. Don't talk so much, don't let others talk to you too much. Talking is a great expenditure of energy.

Here is a technique to help you not to talk excessively: Keep the tip of your tongue curled against the roof of your mouth. Nobody will know what you are doing, it's your secret, but the reminder will be there until the new imprint is set. Also, try to avoid spending hours in front of the television—too many words and too much negativity feeding the brain! Spend time in silence, fully alert and awake. Silence helps to gather and store energy. You owe it to yourself. You already are the One That Is, but your projections have led you astray, through fascination with this world.

It is not necessary to try to become something so fantastic you can't live with yourself. You don't have to act like a saint, whatever that is. Just use awareness as your axis for growth, the central line of development. It's so simple: *We free ourselves by being aware of what we're doing.* If you identify with something, you become it—like an actor with a role. So identify with higher levels, higher beings.

And remember that you are not alone. The cosmos is a hierarchy—there are higher beings above you who will help. Try to dedramatize your worries, be like a little child. Open up to the higher levels. Drop all the "me" and the "mine." Just relax and awaken to the light.

DREAMS

Was it a vision, or a waking dream?

JOHN KEATS

Part of the self leaves the body when we sleep, and changes shape.

RUMI

Dreams are as valid conscious realities as the reality experienced in the outer awake state. . . . Dream realities are far closer to our natural states of Beingness than even the most highly intensified outer reality.

W. BRUGH JOY, M.D.

We speak of the dream-state as being unreal and the waking-state as being real. Strictly speaking, however, both states are unreal, for they depend upon the same order of perceptions.

W. Y. EVANS-WENTZ

We can develop the capacity to be awake in our dreams. . . . Because mindfulness or lucidity seems harder to attain in the dream than in the waking state, practice in lucid dreaming should be especially effective in improving your waking capacity for mindfulness.

STEPHEN LABERGE

Chapter 7

DREAMS

It is easy to say "Awaken," but is life not a dream? And then . . . into what shall we awake?

And dreams—what are they anyway? In Spanish there is a saying: "Dreams are just dreams." This explains nothing, except that it shows us how superficial our concept of "dream" is, and how scared most people are of this dimension. It's like saying, "What is the ocean? Oh, just an expanse of water of which you can't see the end." But what about the depth?

So let us sit at the edge of that ocean which is the dream world. It's not a shore; it's an abyss in which we see no bottom. It's an awe-inspiring immensity in which we pass a good part of our life, and in which we suddenly realize we cannot pinpoint our position.

By entering this research, we soon become part of a dream. It is dreamed by humanity and by our little brothers, the animals. We begin to tune into the silent, infinite world of plants, all ever dreaming their life. And finally, we wonder if our daily problems and reality may be someone's else's dream—or nightmare. At that point we desperately try to recognize a reality, and discover that it is totally relative, with all its pain and joys. We find that our greatest achievements and tragedies lose all value as we shift from one reality to another, and maybe . . . another dream.

Have you noticed that your reality is constantly and gradually changing—loneliness to love, poverty to riches, or vice versa? We try to hold onto our physical world, for we have a craving for reality. But at what point is it stable? At what point is it objective? Do we look and feel at seventy the way we looked and felt at sixteen? Are we still interested in the same "real" things around us? Don't we feel the shift into the dreams? Do we not dream, planning our tomorrows which often never come as they were dreamed? At what point in life can we put down our feet and say, "This is reality and the rest dreams"? Is it when we are happy and we want it to last, or when we are miserable and hit our heads against the bars of our despair?

But now look at it from the *other* side, the dream side. Doesn't it happen exactly like that? In our nightmares, does not our daily reality most often totally vanish? Only the sense of still being "myself" survives through the pain of the nightmare. At that time, where is our house, family, work, and all the details that fill our daily life?

Well, let me explain. The problem is the *state of passivity* we find ourselves in as we slide—generally unaware—into dreams. Like a man overboard in a turbulent sea, we can grasp no handle. We feel we are the object of a strange script.

But reverse that attitude, and the scene changes. How? There is only one way: awareness. Acquire awareness—the awareness of "me" slipping, changing wavelengths, and entering or focusing on a different reality. Just as on your TV, as soon as you change channels, the previous scene disappears *totally*—from a war scene to a romantic love scene in the moonlight—it is another world. This must be kept well in mind.

You may say this seems a very mundane way of explaining very subtle matters, but that is the wonder of life: the beauty of attaining liberty of action on all levels. There is no one basic reality, there are infinite realities. We can live them all, and we must enjoy them all. As wealthy people buy new houses and move from country to country, you can define for yourself the reality you want to inhabit—after having gained the capacity to visit those realities.

Let me suggest that you start your apprenticeship with your *next* dimension. Don't start traveling too far. Your dream world is our actual subject.

Awake or Asleep?

First of all, have you ever noticed that when you enter a dream it is already "on"? It doesn't start with your appearance in it. No one welcomes you to the show or onto the stage, nor is anyone actually waiting for your arrival. It is more like boarding a bus. Each passenger is doing his or her own thing, and you settle down to do yours. And no special sign will appear to say that everything will stop and vanish just because you are awake and come out of it.

The more you work on dreams—the more you practice this travel with awareness—the nearer you come to a lucid dream state in which you realize you really *have* changed dimensions, especially since you are able to compare them. This comes naturally to you. And the first thought is, "Hey, I'm dreaming—this is not my usual world." It is the start of a new, wonderful experience and realization.

But first you must begin by awakening *here*, in the world of your five senses and three dimensions. This is the world that our dear Reason has built for us, the level where we are now, which we call our reality. Don't kid yourself—90 percent of the time you are sound asleep and dreaming, even if you drive at 70 miles an hour. You see, there is only one difference between the so-called real world and the dream world. The first seems to have a *continuity* which gives it credibility. The other is tremendously topsy-turvy; it seems *disconnected* and much more unpredictable and fluid than our daily one.

Let me tell you a story that illustrates this situation. Once upon a time there lived a poor bum who slept every night under the Louvre bridge in Paris, like so many other *clochards*. He was as normal as that kind of life permitted him to be. During the day he rummaged in the local trash, or enjoyed the sunshine along the river Seine. But one night a very peculiar thing started to happen to him, and it continued with uncanny regularity. As soon as he would fall asleep he would dream that he was the king, King Louis XIII, in the palace of the Louvre above him.

As the king he would then go through all the duties of his position. But as soon as he would lay his royal head on the royal pillow for the night's rest, he would open his eyes as the *clochard* and start again his miserable day.

During the first week he was terribly confused. But after a few months he could not distinguish if he was indeed a bum dreaming he was a king, or a king dreaming he was a bum. What made the mystery impenetrable was the logical sequence of events in both roles, the logical continuity of his two existences, the one starting at the moment the other stopped. The two lives were not fragmentary, like dreams, they were continuous; and when we have *continuity*, we take it for reality. So, without any illogical lapse, the poor fellow could not push the wedge of doubt into either existence.

But wait—is a sequence of events necessarily logical?

Well, events for us are the relations we make with what we perceive. We go through life headlong, like a space vehicle into an asteroid belt. But only some of these asteroids hit our senses, the rest go over our head. According to our maturity, culture, interest, and emotional character, we run into many or just very few events. For example, a farmer in the hills of some underdeveloped country has few things happen to him during his lifetime, compared to a rich and handsome woman who is a top executive in a New York corporation.

Next, let us look at the essence of what we call logical events. Whatever philosophical trend we choose, we always have to argue it out with our brain. Our brain cannot think without following its own laws—or, better said, limitations. According to Reason, everything must have a cause, produce an effect, have some sort of duration, and occupy space.

Every time something happens we expect to find a cause. If we cannot, in the back of our mind we are still sure there is one. Meanwhile, we put in its place a symbol—destiny, the will of God, or even "coincidence," which is the flimsiest of them all.

Let's take a real example: A plane left from New York, picked up passengers in another city, and headed for Puerto Vallarta, on the Mexican coast. The passengers included a young couple on their honeymoon, a sports team, and people of all different walks of life, ages, interest, and means, most of them bound for a vacation. The *logical* thing would have been that at least half of them would achieve this goal. It would have been *logical* for the young loving couple, full of plans and hopes, to get to their hotel. But no. The plane crashed against a mountain, and all were killed. Now tell me, is that logical? It is simply absurd. There is not one plan in any of the passenger's heads that conceived as a logical sequence this horrid ending. They obviously considered the risk of crashing, everyone does. But as a logical sequence to anything they had done—no.

Now let's return to the existence of multiple realities. All dimensions have the same mechanics, which can be formulated in a simple aphorism: *At whatever level a consciousness becomes aware, it creates a reality defined by its own limitations.* The center of awareness, then, becomes the vehicle organizing the elements it relates to.

Remember the immense dark field littered with objects? The spotlight of consciousness moves over it, bringing into awareness whatever it lights up. As this awareness/reality moves over the dark field, the rest recedes into oblivion. In fact, cosmically, no object exists. But the *essences* are translated into awareness and relative fields are organized into coherent realities.

I know this vision leaves us with a sense of uneasiness. We have been so used to the illusion of objectivity that being without it makes us feel like children at school the very first time our mother leaves us there. But this is the proof that we are beginning to grow. This is the great difference between the materialistic world view of our forefathers, which we followed as obedient and not very curious children, and our tremendous Void, which we are to recognize as full of life at all the levels of our developing awareness.

Opening Doors into Other Dimensions

Through dreams we can enter into practical contact with what theoretical physics calls our "possibilities." We have several doors to the first dimension beyond the 3-D world in which we act. I will open a few of them for you by means of certain techniques: (1) the nighttime shift into sleep with awareness by recognizing hypnagogic images; (2) the morning exit from the dream level; and (3) the daytime extension beyond the alpha state, where psychiatry has to stop. Of course, as one's consciousness expands, other possibilities will appear.

Recognizing Hypnagogic Images

Prepare for the dreamwork by cleansing. First on the physical level, by cleaning your teeth and hands. Then wash away all your preoccupations. Tell yourself, "The day is over. To each day its own pain and sorrow and worries. Now it's finished . . . I will forget it." Lie on your back, hands at your sides. Breathe in slowly three times to empty the lungs. Breathe in; exhale completely; pause for a time with the air out; then breathe in again. This leads to relaxation.

Then visualize a serene and beautiful scene—a sunset on the ocean, a field of wildflowers, snowy mountains. Perhaps say a prayer that you know. Your state of consciousness will go up, your brain will cool down. Slowly draw the energy up from your toes out through the crown of the head.

Now it is time for some self-hypnosis. Tell yourself, "I will remember my dreams." It isn't enough to say, "I *want*." You need to say, "I *will*." Remembering dreams is the first step toward awareness in the dream state. Over time, as you remember your dreams, you will find a continuity—you will remember more and more. To enforce the self-hypnosis, to fix the intention, visualize a red circle. In the circle see this sentence in big, black letters: "I WILL REMEMBER MY DREAMS." See it clearly. Then let the circle become smaller and smaller until it is a dot.

Now you can watch for the hypnagogic state. You will see moving images behind your eyelids. Thoughts will lose rationality. Here's the tricky part: Before you fall completely asleep, *become aware* that you are slipping into another dimension. Begin to observe a dream.

You should be able to do this every night, unless for some reason you are so tired that you black out totally. As you follow this slipping process, from the normal rational thinking into the unreasonable sequences of dream thoughts, you must admit that either all of humanity goes crazy every night, or indeed we start thinking with another apparatus.

Let's test this assertion. We can always pull out of a dream and wake ourselves back to our normal reasonable state, which proves we don't go crazy. This must mean that we do indeed begin to think with another thinking complex. Dreams are beyond the rational mind—Reason can't accept two minutes of the illogical stuff we dream! What happens is that we shift our awareness to a more subtle level, using the astral blueprint of our brain. And we are never surprised at illogicality in dreams, because we are using the other apparatus, the astral blueprint brain. Now as you slip into the astral world, observe how you shift yourself there and back. The dream is beginning . . . Reason has given up . . . and off you go . . .

The first dreams are lower-level dreams. You know there is a blanket of air around the earth, and its lowest layer is composed of smog and clouds. Just so, our dreams at a low level are based on earthly actions; the higher layers are more subtle, like the ionosphere. The early dreams of the night, eructations of daily events, are of the smoggy level. (Many people mistakenly think all dreams are like this.) After the early dreams, the "garbage" of the lower levels, there is deep sleep and blackout. Then our consciousness begins to perceive higher levels. The dreams we have just before waking are usually these higher, more lucid dreams.

Waking from the Dream State

This exercise is extremely important. Why? Because if you realize it with full awareness, it may lead you to immediate mastery over the death trauma, fear and all. It will also put you face to face with an absolute evidence—with the undeniable fact that we are living among many different, and sometimes not so different levels, or worlds, inhabited by autonomous consciousnesses like you and me.

Have you ever heard it said, "As above, so below"? Just as you may easily cross from the United States into Tijuana, immediately finding another language and set of customs but still meeting human beings, so you can enter (or, better said, tune in to) another dimension. You can be there in a dimension you never imagined and, as I will now guide you to do, experience the most unexpected realities.

Any morning, just before opening your eyes, you may still vividly remember your last dream—that is, still be in it. But at the same time, you may feel that you are at any moment capable of opening your eyes, turning over, and getting out of bed. At this point, *don't move*. If you do, the dream scenery you are still immersed in will waver, as a photo seen through a layer of water—it will waver and vanish. And you will remain "on this side," wide awake, and will start your day.

So don't budge. Keeping your awareness of the daylight coming through your window and the feel of the weight of your bed cover and sheets, slide back into your dream. Now part of the bedroom scenery will dim. Hold onto both if possible. Then resolutely get back into the dream scene and make a change to prove your awareness and control, do something drastic that you would never do in a public place.

For instance, if the scene is a restaurant you were just leaving, go back and turn over a table, or push a man's face into his soup. If you prefer, just take some silverware and run out of the restaurant into the street, like a clumsy thief. You may think this sounds like fun and easy to do, but you may well have a surprise. The characters in your dream are part of the scene. You didn't "think them up," as you would in a daydream adventure where you imagine them doing whatever you want. No, they are there on their own, and they act normally. You will find that doing any unusually drastic thing there is just as difficult as it would be for you here in a "real" restaurant. It will take all your guts—although you are still aware you are in your bed, and can get out of this embarrassing situation at will.

But why does it take guts? We can usually imagine any story, see ourselves acting in it, without any fear or emotion. Why not in this particular case? Simple: This dream world has absorbed your total personality—except the physical vehicle in bed, which just keeps on functioning on the autonomic level handled by the cerebellum. "You," with all your values, are in the other world of the lucid dream, a world so near to ours that it is almost like a photocopy. Most of our moral and social values are valid there, and that's what makes you feel so uneasy when you do something drastic. You have reentered their level, and the people there are just like you—human types, not your imaginary characters—so you can't foresee their reactions at all. The whole thing will now become so real it is scary; but as you have the choice to remain in the dream and face unpleasant consequences, or just turn tail and run—you open your eyes, turn over, and laugh it off with a sigh. Wow, it's over, I'm back home!

This important adventure will teach you, through the evidence of your own experience, that we have neighbors in a neighboring dimension. It will also teach you that with awareness you may modify that world, or at least the part you enter, with your actions and will power. And last but not least, it will teach you that the physical body is not indispensable to your existence. If for any reason your heart should have stopped beating while you were "there," you could have carried on perfectly well. In that dimension your own (and their) limitations provide you with a physical body exactly like the one in bed, though maybe healthier and younger. What I mean by "provide" is, of course, that both you and your "neighbors" cannot conceive of a person without a body, clothes, and so forth. And the characteristics of the self-image that you project define the quality of your clothes, appearance, and bearing. That's why we, and others, often "see" ourselves as younger and more vibrant than we are.

You may ask, "Who are these people?" Hard to say. First of all, we tune in to wavelengths of our own kind—this is called *syntony*. These vibrations are very close to each other like the slightest turn of the knob on a radio. So some are human travelers astray in that frequency, as if they had mistaken one street for another. Others may be humans who have died and cannot define their level. And others may be mental forms produced by authors, like movie characters who never made it into the camera but remain full of emotional energy, acting the part that they "should" have enacted in the mind of the author. They are very real at this semi-astral level.

If you permit me a little side trip, I'll tell you of an interesting case. It happened in a very exclusive group of "spirit" researchers back in 1925, when that sort of research was at its height of popularity. They used a medium who possessed the talent of exudating sufficient etheric energy out of his body when he was in a trance state to permit an entity to present itself, plasmating with a physical body. (This etheric energy is called ectoplasm. It has weight, 9 grams, and a very low temperature, 29 degrees centigrade.) These very rare apparitions do not materialize their legs and feet, but appear—in the center of the circle formed by the researchers holding hands—only down to the middle of their thighs. In fact, when an apparition wants to communicate through direct voice, as it is called, not the voice of the medium, it must obviously create with the ectoplasm it has been given by the medium, a larynx, palate, and teeth, plus a tongue. Otherwise it would be howling, not speaking intelligibly.

So, the group had the satisfaction and excitement to have at each weekly session the manifestation of a young man. His appearance was characteristic of a sick person—pale features, unkempt hair—and his speech was constantly interrupted by a painful cough. His clothes were definitely of 1830, the Romantic period. He presented himself by name, by profession as poet, and then through weekly seances narrated the "true" story of his life, love, and death.

My master, Tulio Castellani, was part of this research group. He decided to go and check on the ailing apparition. And, briefly, this was the result, to the great disillusion of the spiritists: The "spook" had never existed as a human. He was the main character of a romantic novel of the 1880s, and the characteristics which he gave were clearly defined in the novel. If Tulio hadn't been a mathematician, entomologist, physicist, and lawyer, with his head firmly planted on his shoulders, he would have swallowed this astral hoax and everyone would have been feeding this entity with vital energy, as compassion and love went out to the poor astral liar.

If there is one world where lying seems to be the main activity, it is the astral. So beware of its visitors! They are great impersonators, because of the fluid energy/matter they manipulate. They may wear cloaks, turbans, have a nice tan, oriental eyes, and a patriarchal presence. And if you give them a chance, they will appear in your dreams. They may transmit love and respect. But many of these masquerading entities are outright psychic vampires who "feed" on human energy in order not to evaporate, to dissolve into their medium like gelatin in warm water. So if you haven't any defense, keep away from them.

If you encounter darkness in a dream, or something which is horrible to you, you can confront it with a religious symbol or phrase. A cross, a Buddhist *mantram*, whatever is most natural for you. This is in itself an exercise in awareness, and therefore valuable for your development.

As for the interpretations of dreams, replay them *without emotion* and the symbols will drop off; that is, freeze your emotional/astral and they will appear like line drawings, without color. You will then be able to see what they mean. Remain quiet and contemplative. Our dreams are like frames cut from a film. You can't understand a whole film by seeing a few feet cut out of the middle! In the same way, we see only parts of the dream reality. So look for the essence of the dream.

Beyond the Alpha State

The alpha state technique is quite interesting and rather easy to try. Its basis is the normal, juvenile habit of "daydreaming." This simply means sitting *comfortably*, and letting your mind roam in search of some pleasant adventure that you imagine or "make up."

The difference with the previous technique of dream reentry is that here we consciously sit down and invent, well aware we are doing it, creating the props and characters of our adventure.

Get comfortable in your armchair or sofa. Don't use your bed—you don't want to fall asleep, as you would then enter the dream state without autonomy, as one usually does during the night. Now close your eyes and imagine, for example, that a charming person who is sexually attractive to you enters the room. Make up your scenery, but keep it very simple—bare walls, a large bay window looking out on a garden. So: He or she enters. Greetings, looks, affectionate embrace—you are both very near and happy—and you may start imagining that a love affair is developing. (Mind you, this is all willfully made up by your imagination.) Up to this point, any teenager does it. It's easy and fun.

But now, while you are kissing, out of the corner of your eye look at the scenery, the props. You might well discover that the room has changed. On that wall, which you did not imagine in detail, a painting with a gilded frame has appeared. Further down, there on your left, is a door, and you can see it leads to other rooms. A furtive silhouette just flashed by. What is happening?

What happened is that you just crossed the border again. You primed the pump by starting to make up an adventure, knowing quite well you did it, that it wasn't there at all. But as you created the setting, as your physical sensations vanished because of your restful position, your focus drifted off toward the alpha dream level. Without noticing the border, you just slipped into the astral dimension.

Now you and your dream lover are on your own. Just take your lover's hand and lead him or her backstage, so to speak, and enter into the dream world in full awareness. Let things happen. With practice you can evoke other beings, create other settings at will instantaneously. These settings will need no imagining, just watching. They belong to a subtle energy field and will unroll spontaneously around you as a totally unexpected world, autonomous, real, and beyond your control, except for immediate details.

You will be able to create these experiences by expanding your consciousness through the doors of inner silence. And this growth of awareness beyond the normal limits will "bleed out" to your daily capacities, empowering you in this world, and introducing you to the final solution of Life and Death.

You will also learn one of the ever-present laws of the cosmos: *The power of creation descends from the subtle to the concrete.* That is already clear in the gospel of St. John, where the Word—the precise image of an idea—is equal to, the same as, the Creator. From then on the creation develops as preset and preexisting in the original concept—the Word.

All this should give you a hint. It is from *behind* the props on stage that the scenery can be modified. The spectators—people in daily life—see only the effect. Your empowerment caused by expansion of consciousness into other levels is the key to the modification of what appears as "material reality." Try to wear out the skin of "reality" to the point where you go right through it.

WHAT IS DEATH?

The fear of death is the fine for accepting the identity of the body as a separate entity in the total functioning.

NISARGADATTA

There is no Death! What seems so is transition.

HENRY WADSWORTH LONGFELLOW

If you are afraid of death you can escape that fear by believing in reincarnation, but fear is still there . . . Concepts do not help get rid of fear.

KRISHNAMURTI

There is no death, only a change of awareness, a change of cosmic address.

BOB TOBEN

His good works receive him who has done good and has gone from this world to the other—as friends and kinsmen receive a traveler on his return.

TEACHINGS OF THE BUDDHA

Chapter 8

WHAT IS DEATH?

From our detailed understanding of dreams, and our practice of extension into other dimensions, we are naturally led to the so-called problem of death. Here let us take a necessary pause: Death is not problematic, but it is, for humans, a mystery. Doesn't it seem extraordinary that with our thousands of years of history, surrounded by people, animals, and plants that are born, manifest themselves during their lives, and finally die that we, the actors and observers, still consider this natural phenomenon a real mystery play?

The mystery for us is not the way death may happen (we always find that out, you know) but *when*—and, very specifically, what will be the next act, if any. This "if any" has bugged humanity for quite a while.

But has it always been that way? Did other civilizations also grope in the dark, facing this experience?

What the ancient civilizations thought about death has been brought to our knowledge through two channels. First, the historical, comprising descriptions of ancient philosophies; second, all the Esoteric schools, sects, cults, and oriental infiltrations. But the doubtful side of the historical, officially accepted descriptions is that they have all been brought to us (alas, for our understanding!) filtered, mashed, and processed to a pulp according to the limits of the processing tool. Unfortunately, this tool has been tailored by at least three hundred years of a deepening materialistic mindset of the most unpractical, moronic type. As for the

Esoteric information, it is often dangerously confusing because it has come to us as a cascade of oriental wisdom, shipped in barrels permeated by the taste of Judeo-Christian vintage: The whole concoction is therefore composed of several contradicting belief systems, mixed with cool-headed techniques and slobbery, emotional, popular Yogas.

The rational computer will give us no answer to the post-mortem mystery. Reason never receives any data from beyond the sensory curtain. Since at death the instrument itself is dissolved, where do we expect it to get its information from?

It is much more difficult for a normal, intelligent person to achieve evidences about the after-death state than it is for a self-educated person to become a multimillionaire. We make money using our conventional rational system, but metarational experiences need a very fine tuning up of special brain circuits. These circuits are not yet normally ours, according to the evolutionary program of dear Mother Nature. You must make a quantum leap of at least two hundred years, as it's still beyond Homo sapiens. Since I, among others, have made the leap, I will report my results to you. Let's get down to brass tacks.

We all live in a fine bionic machine. Doctors know, theoretically, how it "should" run, and they usually try their best to keep it that way, or to repair the repairable. When the mechanism gets beyond that stage, through wear and tear or accident, it stops working.

The physical aspects of death—the throes, agony, rigidity—are just for the onlookers, whose suffering is in direct proportion to their lack of spiritual preparation. We know by experience that as soon as we feel sleepy, our brain loses its sharpness. And when we are falling asleep, the change in blood flow to our brain shuts off the five sense channels, and we black out. This also happens when we feel too much pain—it is an escape switch, a conditioned automatism, or reflex. Therefore, when consciousness is lost, all the twisting, panting, and moaning remains as a terrifying spectacle for the onlooker, who naturally identifies himself with the dying person, now in fact far beyond pain. When we watch our dear ones as they die we go through excruciating anguish and despair, we feel our heart is broken.

But that is from this side of the sensory curtain. The continuity of the action is behind it, behind the "props" of the five senses, and very much less dramatic. As we who watch cannot perceive anything beyond these five senses, one or more deathbed experiences of this kind may well destroy our will to live, to love again, and to function in our worldly society. And rightly so, as when you have lost your beloved child or companion, you feel there are really very few things left worth any sustained effort.

I am not trying to belittle our human sorrows (which are so often shared by our poor, loving pets). Remember, I do not pretend to have received what knowledge I may have by some divine grace, nor am I some *bodhisattva* arrived on this planet on a golden cloud to save humanity. No, my friends, I come from the human rank and file, and have matured through tears and suffering amid many who also wept and suffered. This is the reason for my struggle for freedom from the human condition of existence, and my goal in life to liberate those who are willing to experiment with the tools for liberation. Nor do I pretend to have invented the tools. They have been given me by highly matured beings who considered me worthy of receiving them to serve others, since I had, as it is said in Esoteric scrolls, "washed my feet with the blood of my heart" before stepping on the Path.

The constant unpredictability of the human drama led me to the experiences through which one can finally understand death. But just as the modern quantum physicists in their search for the building blocks of "matter," fell right through and found themselves in the void, so my search for the reality of death led me through the labyrinth of illusion. To the cry, "There is no matter!" answers the echo: "There is no death!"

That's what I want you to see with me through these pages. And if you are one of the willing, I will give you the keys to the dimensions.

Science and Death

First let us look at the map. Until the sixteenth century all these questions relating to the soul, death, and their consequences were answered by the authority of the church. As these answers handed out to the people gave them a lot of consolation and kept them more or less out of mischief, it was politically okay. But a minority was pragmatically inclined. For them these explanations just didn't make it. So they undertook a new (for the West, at least) philosophical research. It began with what was, for them, evident: their five senses. And so it was called "sensism." From sensism to pragmatism to materialism, the whole thing became a lifestyle, a vision of the evident world, in German a *Weltanschauung*. This way of seeing the world helped to develop rational power, and so we ended up with our mechanistic, materialistic view of the world. All this functioned well. It promoted colonialism, profitable wars, and heavy industry, and rolled history along to the clanging of pistons and cogs until Albert Einstein spilled the beans with relativity.

From then on it really became a bad trip. Relativity, you see, shakes up our comfortable, static time-space concept. Suddenly, things that go fast become shorter! You just ride them (if you can!) and you stop aging! Space (so beautifully blue) is curved, and if you can (again!) go as fast as light you might end up in bed with Cleopatra.

As their cosmos shook and trembled, the old-timers retired into the refuge of their feeding grounds, the universities; but the furies of progress had been let loose. Even Albert, the antennae of his genius perceiving harder times to come, cried out: "No, there must be a solution. God does not play dice with the universe." He then died, and we must hope that he reached his synthesis beyond the blackboard. But his colleagues remained in a fix: Today, through the explosion of quantum physics, the world of matter has vanished into oblivion.

None of these revolutionary concepts, however, will enter into the minds of average people before a good century has passed. Eventually, their children—by studying on computers and handling electronic gadgetry of all kinds—will grow the brain circuits to begin to understand.

Even so, it will probably remain translated only at the rational level. Just as for the past three centuries the concept of matter versus spirit was an *evidence,* the coming generations will follow in the usual groove before reaching transcendental comprehension—although they already manipulate forces which cannot be measured through even the most sensitive detectors.

A good example is the emanations of crystals. The evidence is there: Algae will vanish in a swimming pool if a crystal is present. This is much faster than chlorine, and much safer for the eyes. But as the cause cannot be followed up to the effect logically, the rational computer is at a loss, running around in circles like a dog chasing its tail. A crystal emits no chemical from which we can trace a reaction. What it emits is an imperceptible force field, still scientifically undetectable. This being unexplainable, Reason applies the good old aphorism: "It cannot be, therefore it isn't!" And . . .*tutti contenti.*

But as usual, it's a case of "the dogs bark, but the caravan passes."

These old parameters are the ones under which the phenomenon of death has been and is still being evaluated. It's an excellent evaluation for a mortician or the coroner; but they see only a corpse to be treated and measured, not the totality. The holistic vision is beyond them.

Now let us look at death scientifically. Not in the Newtonian way, but according to high-energy physics.

The good old bewhiskered materialists gave the physical body priority as to reality. What was real was physical. Not the sentiments, or a supposed soul, or mere thoughts. All this they derided as nonsensical superstitions, arguments for priests or sentimental old maids. Practical, scientific minds would stick to material facts.

But please follow me here: When I was a small boy I loved my father as much as I do today, although he died fifty years ago. My sentiments are constantly renewed through memory, and my maturity through aging, now that I am eighty-one. In my mind his image has not changed, and his qualities are better understood. But what has happened to my physical body—the gold standard of reality for the pragmatic materialist? Oh dear! First of all, not one cell of the ten-year-old boy is still in this old body of mine. Since our cells are completely renewed every ten years, mine have changed eight times.

So who is it who is still loving Papa? Me? Who is that? Believe me, no one in the world who had known me at ten could ever recognize me now at eighty-one! And as a matter of fact, my physical body cannot love or hate anything or anybody. It has no direct contact with sentiments, it can only react to them, not produce them—that is a job for the subtle vehicles. Look at any number of the unfortunate people stricken by mental disorders from birth. Or a comatose "body"—to what does it respond?

So who is loving Papa? My memory? My sentiments? Hold it! All this is not real by materialistic standards, all this is abstract. The facts are that the so-called real Andrew who loves Papa has vanished eight times totally. And each time he sort of got himself together again to pay his taxes, even Papa would never have recognized him.

Look at what happens here. We have a physical "reality." But, as we saw in the last chapter, what for us is "real" *must* have an underlying continuity or lose its characteristic of reality. And this physical "reality" has switched roles! The "immaterial" (loving Papa) continues steadily through eighty years, and the "material" (the body) becomes as fluid as a flowing river—the water of which is never the same but is still called a river for the sake of convenience.

If you think seriously about this physical body, there is no reason to be surprised about its maleability, as it's made of changing energy fields. But our forefathers were certain that the body was matter—not knowing that matter is a cloud of vibrating energy and nothing else—so they stood by the matter concept. And they deduced every argument from that belief. As usual, when a premise is false, the deductions will also be false, and these have caused, during the last two thousand years, an ocean of tears and pain.

I must repeat: We are made of energy, and we vibrate in a cosmos of energy fields. Therefore, if we could for an instant reduce our size to that of an atom, our bodies—now "matter" for us at our human scale and size—would appear to us like so many Milky Ways! Each atom—and don't forget that an atom is just a vibrating frequency, nothing perceivable for our senses—is separated from its nearest neighbor by huge distances, very much like our planetary systems. And between them? Nothing but the Void.

So we should not be surprised that we change so much. The body, put together in the womb from a desire for manifestation, follows the psychosomatic blueprint of the species. And after completion it is evicted at birth. It grows and ages. And, after suffering for three-quarters of a century the disrupting impacts of negative emotions, our body is forcibly modified by cellular replacements and becomes, finally, hardly recognizable. In simple words, when the baby becomes an old man of seventy-five, he looks like God knows what!

Death and the Soul

We can no longer pretend to take such a perishable and fluid element for the standard of reality. We shall have to look elsewhere.

What will our next standard be? Although we humans live in a constant everywhere-now, this is not apparent to our senses, and therefore is not apparent to Reason. The unpredictability of life reflects itself on our characters. It is because of this endemic fear of the unknown that we are constantly looking for reality, for security, for something to hold on to. And many of us gladly surrender our liberty to the enslavement of jobs, military ranks, or the laws of some divinity, in order to feel *terra firma* under our hesitating feet.

We just said we must reach out for something more firm than an organized field of magnetic forces that appears solid only at our level of perception, and which is ever changing and condemned to dissolution. Clearly, we have lost matter forever. And so, holding onto *continuity* as our only reality, we have to lean upon the only element we can experience every day, and that is our electromagnetic complex or vehicle of emotions and desires: our astral body, or soul.

We have seen that this element has the possibility of continuity. Our passions—political, patriotic, or scientific, for instance—can last for a lifetime, and even be contagious and hereditary.

But here we also find a problem of continuity. Supposing I am madly in love with Mary. When I think of Mary I will feel the glow of sharing the warmth of love. But what happens when, under stressful circumstances, my consciousness shifts its focus onto the urgency and means of solution of a newly born problem—a multiple car crash on a freeway, for instance? During that half hour, for me, Mary has just ceased to exist! My consciousness-awareness, like a spotlight, has shifted its beam for a given time.

"Oh no," we can say, "that does not mean I suddenly have stopped loving Mary. She is in my memory bank. As soon as the problem is solved, she will be, I am sure, the first thought that will come to my mind."

At this point we are not facing a sentimental or moral issue, but a life-and-death issue. Let us remember we are trying to pinpoint an element that would be equivalent to our ancient concept of reality, something like our idea of a physical body enduring as such through our life, which we have found to be an illusion.

Now we find that the more subtle vehicle we may call astral or soul, which we hoped would substitute for material reality, has as many holes as a slice of Swiss cheese! At the moment of my accident I may have had an image of Mary waiting at home for me, then I turned back to the crash scene in which I was involved. But Mary might quite well have leaned over the balcony looking for my return, and toppled over, killing herself on impact. What happens then?

Look out, look out! Don't fall back on the materialistic level of thinking again. Mary's body was not her totality, and the *continuity* of Mary consists of the same elements to which our love and harmony always vibrated. But if I am an average man, unprepared, in losing Mary's body I have lost it all.

Our expectation of reality can be justified only if we can follow a trend of continuity as it winds through a holistic universe. We lose the thread of continuity when we cannot change levels in *full awareness*; through the impact of pain, we remain stuck in a given dimension. We forget that when we focus on one relative reality, let's say our 3-D world, another, the astral, becomes an abstraction. And in turn, our 3-D world becomes an abstraction as soon as we change focus to the astral.

Continuity is easy on subtle levels, because the subtle bodies suffer less wear and tear. The fact that the material world is relative does not mean there is no permanent life. But, as we said, we lack a certain agility to change focus. And this leads us back to the root of the subject: Awareness, the key to all powers which we have not yet realized for lack of inner silence, Awareness, the door to other worlds.

The moment we understand that our body is the vehicle and not the driver, death loses its mystery and becomes a terrain of extremely interesting experiences which we can reach through the right techniques. As the remaining vehicles suffer no wear and tear, we find ourselves in a continuity without anxiety—the anxiety that time is passing, that there is insufficient time. This serene sense of continuity reflects itself through onto our daily activity and also creates the ideal conditions for a sane and active longevity, so important to family life. The frantic search for security gives way to a powerful sense of stability. Through the entry into inner silence we begin to hear the voice of Mother Earth, stability itself! It permeates all our concrete daily decisions and begins creating empowerment, the growth of a feeling of invulnerability, of a certainty that our efforts will give the right fruit.

Sleep and Death

In Greek mythology, sleep and death appear as twins. As you

can now recognize, this symbology was very apt. The loss of the physical vehicle, which we call death, is the disconnection of all the vital elements—emotions, thoughts, and so forth—which are "us" from that vehicle, a disconnection quite similar to sleep.

Let's look at an example. We take the love of our companion for granted on Monday. And we can rightly expect it to be the same on Tuesday, and so on. But if we ask our beloved when she is sound asleep, "Darling, do you love me?" what do we get for an answer? Silence, or maybe a grunt. Why? Because our loved one is elsewhere. She has focused her "I am" on another level, or world, and who can tell if she is or isn't having a passionate love affair on that level with someone else? "Ah," you may say, "it's just a dream."

Is it? Our awareness of one level erases another. Our awareness on one is not guaranteed on the next. She is not responsible; as at that moment she probably has no memory of her home, or you!

So, you see, sleep is an excellent imitation of death. The recycling process is laid bare for us to see: one awareness to another, one day to another, one life to another, no remembrance.

Of course for most people, who are not informed or trained in the disciplines we have talked about, death is a final end. The physical body with which they totally identify, once deprived of its vital elements, suddenly begins dissolving and returning each chemical element that composed it to its own cosmic source. This vision is usually terrifying and repulsive and accounts for the fear of the corpse. All of this, as I have said, takes place on our side of the drama, the sensory experience.

As to the rest of the activity, which takes place on more subtle levels—the extension of the awareness of the so-called dead persons to other experiences—it has nothing to do with the drama of the 3-D level at all, which at the moment of death vanishes for a given period.

There is an exception for some people who are totally identified with the body. Those who were raised in a materialistic family (chosen by affinity with their prenatal tendencies) are so persuaded that they *are* their physical entity, they cannot easily detach themselves from the corpse, which they feel as the only way of existence. These unfortunate beings often try to reenter this physical form, and of course have horrifying experiences. Those who loved them and preceded them into the astral do try to help them.

In fact, I did this myself: Three years after the death of my father, for whom I had unbounded love and admiration, I managed to enter into the middle astral levels and found him. But I never could bring him to the awareness that he had "died." This concept has no value in the astral, as the whole level is throbbing with activity, and the word "death" has no translation into a state of consciousness. Remember that in this material world a concept, like death, creates emotions and a state of consciousness. The reverse happens in the astral—everyone there feels evidently alive; death is not understood.

Karma and Death

One fact most people never seem to consider is that for the same reason there are no two identical lives, there are no two identical deaths nor post-mortem experiences. Death is not a phenomenon apart from life, but its prolongation in different conditions—just as our life, our capacity to act, and our interests when we were two years old are quite different from the ones we have today. After all, to a person who last saw us when we were two and reencounters us when we are forty, we might just as well have died and reincarnated. As to what happened to us between two and forty, it is out of that person's reach; while for us our life has continued without interruption. Therefore any answer to the question "What is the after-death experience?" would always have to be an individual experience and can never be generalized.

However, we have our minds, genes, and chromosomes so imbued by the "retribution" syndrome, and we are as a rule so thirsty for justice, that the mere thought of someone getting away with past crimes or cruelty once on the "other side" sets our emotions in turmoil. We may become convinced that there is no justice anywhere. And we humans have a tremendous need for a just Divinity, for judgments, hells, and paradises. So here we meet the law of *karma,* which comes from the East.

Most of us who were brought up in the Judeo-Christian tradition consider that there are "sins"—actions that are against the moral law of a given religion. Fine. If there is sin, there is a law that has been broken. Therefore we have a Divinity that creates laws, evaluates actions and sins, so perforce we have retribution.

In the East, the concept of sin does not exist. The eastern idea of a divinity is of one preoccupied with vast cosmic affairs, who therefore has created the law of *karma* to take care of worldly justice.

Karma is action and reaction, a natural terrestrial phenomenon. It also is the law of *cause and effect.* So, no sin. Instead of sin, the admission of technical errors, which will bring consequences, good or bad. So if you goof . . . you pay! It is as simple as that. Now, when the payment date is depends on circumstances and time. This involves the idea of reincarnation, which in turn involves another problem spiritualists don't like to mention—lack of memory, which we have discussed earlier.

Karma is a respected law that has been bowed to by thousands of millions of people through the ages, and Westerners are taking to it like ducks to water. But if you have an inquiring mind you will soon see that we are in a hell of a mess: It so happens that the category of cause, called causality in general, and which is essential to *karma,* has just been torpedoed and sunk in the sea of quantum physics.

Furthermore, these disciplines will show you that there are no definable final causes. There is generally an evident primary cause, then secondary causes, plus concomitant causes, and so on and so on backwards until we end up with Adam and Eve bickering with the snake.

In other words, if Adolf became a bad guy, it was because Papa and Frau Hitler had genes and chromosomes of their own, inherited from their papas and mamas, with a touch of *Furor Teutonico.* Adolf's actions were therefore conditioned to deviate one way or another, probably the wrong way, and he "couldn't help it."

So where do we pinpoint the cause of Hitler's actions? I don't mean to say everything went okay—what I am getting at is that Adolf is a fine jolt to the law of *karma*. Because this way we might end up like some creeds who tell us that woman is "wicked" because Eve accepted the donation of an apple from a dissident snake. Don't you feel it's stretching culpability a bit far? You see, if we can't define the responsibility of a culprit, how can we define the punishment?

The Laws of Syntony

By now it may seem more evident to you why I generally speak of philosophers with tongue-in-cheek criticism. Whatever we concoct in our minds is so drastically conditioned by the limits of the instrument itself that there is no reason to argue "about it and about," as Omar Khayyám put it, because it has very little to do with cosmic reality. We throw the grid of time, space, cause, effect upon what we perceive, sort out what we put together accordingly, and Abracadabra, we have a cosmology! This is why the Buddha, when asked certain profound metaphysical questions, answered them with his famous "noble silence"—which, by the way, must have been rather maddening. Why answer? It was all "between the ears" of the inquirer!

So what is the solution? There is an old Italian saying: "He who wants, goes. He who doesn't want, sends." In other words, you'd better do it yourself. We are back to our basics again: inner silence, the door through the "white hole" into our other dimensions.

Having comprehended the phenomenology of sleep and our participation in it (which is after all a rehearsal of dying but without traumatic external effects), those who have entered through the door of inner silence will feel more at home in this experience of dying if they have practiced what we may call "traveling the dimensions"—even if the first experience was just going to the border and back.

I hope you have understood that life and death is a continuity with a change of clothes. We abandon our old pink scuba wetsuit and go "skinny dipping" in other frequencies. When you know the techniques you can even follow those you love who have come to the end of their trip, and dive in. In the beginning you will only enter into partial contact with their dimension, because the activity of your body is still very demanding—the attention of the autonomous nervous system, digestive and thermic, plus the energy to make it all go. Therefore, always keep this in mind during your experiences: You will feel sluggish, slowed down, as if you are riding a bicycle that is hauling a heavy cart.

At the loss of the scuba suit you suddenly fly off, and everything at your level becomes bright, clear, and weightless. The first thing to know is that, very much like in our 3-D world, we function through affinity. But our astral vehicle is far more subtle than our physical one, and what it has been composed of during "life" can weigh it down to very slow vibrations. Light is the highest frequency, so at a low level of vibrations there is little or no light—something like the ocean deeps.

Better said: People who load themselves with meanness, egocentricity, hatred, and greed are themselves vibrating very slowly, and are the kind of people one wouldn't want for buddies. In other words, they have become "made" of darkness. This also means that the energy of the cosmos, the speed of which can range from the fastest—light—to the slowest—mineral—corresponds to the scale of vibration of their astral vehicle, or soul. They will at death "tune in" at a given point in this scale according to their specific weight, automatically, as soon as they lose the shell that protects them. Just see it this way: When you swim with your scuba suit, you don't worry about water temperature because you are isolated from the water. But take your suit off in the ocean, and you become the temperature around you.

As we always look for light from "above" and at stones and rocks "below," it begins to be easy to recognize in all this some good old symbols that religions used in order to illustrate their teachings.

The rocks and minerals, in general, are the astral inferior level. Inferior, or low, in Latin is *inferus*, from which come *infernus*, infernal—better said hell! Doesn't this ring a bell?

So for you, my dear future traveler of the dimensions, according to how much ballast you can free yourself of, you will burst out into the light or sink into the depths of the cosmic frequencies. If you are full of love, joy, serenity, and inner silence, the harmony of the spheres, light and bliss are yours! And if you have any buddies who lost their scuba suits but held onto the heavy weights of personal hatreds, vengeances, and the like, during all their lives, you definitely can't follow them, and you will never meet them again.

This statement, which in some cases may be tragic, needs some explanation, which I will give you from my own experience. At the beginning of my inner disciplines my master, Tulio Castellani, knew I would finally turn out to be the "good guy" he was aware that I had to be—but first of all he sent me to the cleaners. There is not much I want to say about myself then. I was a violent young man, with violent past lives. I had always been attracted to the military monastic groups through history—the Knights Templar, later the *samurai* in Japan. And as a naval captain I specialized in submarine weapons during World War II, when I met him. I followed up with the underground, and joined the U.S. forces after Monte Cassino. So I wasn't the goody-goody you might expect.

Castellani put me through a ruthless cleansing process. As one lifetime could never have whitewashed this charming soul of mine, I was offered an option: to pay the effects caused by my past through endless incarnations, or pay now by installments. I chose the latter. Every night I was pushed "down" in syntony with my past actions, into the mineral levels, to serve others and to understand how foolish I had been. Every morning I woke up sweating with horror. But finally, after eight full years, I sweated it all out and didn't suffer any more.

Let me go over once more the basic concept of "going down" or slowing our frequencies to an identity of tone with the mineral world. Light is the outgoing, *centrifugal* cosmic love. It creates manifested life forms, a practical love expanding on all levels. Lack of love, negative activity, indifference to the suffering of others, is *centripedal.* It concentrates, condenses, therefore "materializes" more and more accretions to the "I," attention to what is "mine," for "me."

The more one's energy condenses toward one central focusing point, the slower the vibrations become, until they can find no similar syntony at any manifested "living" level, such as that of animals and plants. They can only covibrate with the extremely slow mineral world, the dynamics of which we cannot even perceive with our senses. Crystals are alive and grow, probably one-thirty-second of an inch in 200,000 to 300,000 years. And don't forget we can't even see plants grow—we have to use time-lapse photography.

Let us postulate a negative, selfish, violent man. While he inhabits his human organism, he is partly his body, but also partly his slowly compacting mental and astral vehicles.

At the moment of death these last two bodies, having lost the sheath they used for contacting the 3-D world, instantly syntonize with the medium they usually vibrated to and are no longer isolated from. Only the mineral world is sufficiently condensed to offer an identity of tone to that kind of mental-astral entity. As light frequencies are the opposite—the fastest—our negative friend feels himself brutally slowed down, precipitated into darkness. (Have you ever had a nightmare in which you were trying to escape but couldn't run? You felt as if you were struggling through deep sand? That's it—you happened to drop a couple of levels!)

His consciousness is still perfectly aware and translates in images all the feelings that are produced by the medium in which he covibrates. Remember, he grew during gestation in his mother's womb a condensed replica (physical brain) of his actual (virtually ever-lasting) astral blueprint brain. He now functions with that one. (We use the term "brain," but please think of it rather as an extremely expanded electronic apparatus vibrating on the wavelength of his individual capacity. The astral brain may not have the incisive acuity of the physical one, and certainly it doesn't follow the cause-and-effect/time/space system necessary for our condensed terrestrial experience. But it is not fuzzy, no more than it is during a nightmare, where everything feels solid and real—even if maybe not logical. This astral "brain" follows a process of coherence, not logic. Happenings are coherent to the man's awareness, sufficiently so never to be doubted, thus giving him the intense sense of realism we have all experienced during nightmares.)

The world of hellish experiences after death is not made of the famous flames and devils. The desires are the devouring "flames" and the "devils" our constant nagging, unsatisfied manias. But we can translate them because of our superstitions into real flames and devils. The frequencies are so tremendously slow that they slow down any thought and action. Generally speaking, normal people finally "purge" themselves (the purgatory of the Christians) or "sweat out" these situations through the incredible effort it takes to move anything in such a sticky, condensed energy field—it is like swimming in tar!

So as unprepared people slip into this stage after the loss of their bodies, they enter into covibration with their *own* frequency level, tuning into it automatically. All the ordinary efforts they employed to survive during "life" are multiplied, tied down, weighed down by the sluggish medium, where every second is equivalent to years of our 3-D world. Everything is a billion times more inaccessible, more unattainable.

It's like a drab, cold, northern European city in the middle of the night—dismally depressing. Housing, work, friends, all in a dark atmosphere of a continuous winter (lack of light), in towns full of brutal aggression, violent oppression by hidden authorities, complex impossible laws—no love, no tenderness, no affection, where even your own dog hates you and growls. It is hell indeed!

But how? Why? All through ignorance, as all of this is but a *trans-*

lation of states of low consciousness-vibrations into *images* by the astral brain (the prenatal blueprint.) None of all of this really exists anywhere. One thought of love, one moment of reverence, would shoot this suffering soul up to the light!

But did our negative friend ever manifest reverence? Wasn't his whole life full of selfishness, arrogance, and sarcasm for those who defended moral, altruistic values? Big fish eats little fish! That was his law. Get smart, take advantage of the credulous, and get what you want out of life. All right, if this was his creed he cannot change it just because he changed his pink leather jacket.

"How long," you may ask, "before he might be redeemed?"

I couldn't tell you. But I can assure you, through my own painful experiences, that as states of consciousness create the vibrations, high or low—and his are low, surrounded by hellish beings in the same condition—I really don't see how our negative friend can suddenly become full of love and peace.

Now, the same laws of syntony prevail for another person, a woman, whose life, let us suppose, has been nonaggressive, whose tendency has always been to stretch out a hand instead of grabbing, or cynically withholding. This kind person, who without pretenses of saintliness has kept a healthy sense of humor about our human fallacies and errors, will enter a level of serene harmony. At the last moment, even if she may be overcome with a sense of sadness when thinking of the ones she leaves behind, her departure will be as a silent explosion of light. Hers is an outgoing heart, not an egocentric one, so she will enter in syntony with the currents of love and compassion.

Harmony is translated by our astral brain (and our physical one also) as beauty. Therefore she will be surrounded by images of love, compassion, and unity with light. Harmonious shapes of color, monuments of musical bliss, the infinite joy of animal and plant souls, and all the elementals of the cosmic dance will be vibrating all around and through her, since she is constructed of the same frequencies.

As you see, all this has been floating through human history as legends, beliefs, and religious teachings, so simplified that they became infantile and lost credibility. But almost all individuals—for reasons of ballast, attachments, or even terrestrial love—return to manifestation. Although without a clear memory, they hold on to these glimpses of happiness and bliss which on the high levels are the definite reality, and have branded on their astral being, so to speak, something "heavenly"—something unforgettable.

INNER ALCHEMY

There is no enduring, permanent personality—Spirit is not anyone's possession. It is the common denominator, that in which we all share, and this alone is permanent and eternal.

TEACHINGS OF THE BUDDHA

It is so self-conscious, so apparently moral, simply to step aside . . . saying, I never merited this grace, quite rightly, and then to sulk along the rest of your days on the edge of rage. I won't have it. The world is wilder than that in all directions, more dangerous and bitter, more extravagant and bright.

ANNIE DILLARD

Attachment is that which dwells upon pleasure. Aversion is that which dwells upon pain . . . Aversion is a form of bondage. We are tied to what we hate or fear. That is why, in our lives, the same problem, the same danger or difficulty, will present itself over and over again in various prospects, as long as we continue to resist or run away from it instead of examining it and solving it.

PATANJALI

Non-attachment may come very slowly . . . it should never be thought of as an austerity . . . The practice of non-attachment gives value and significance to even the most ordinary incidents of the dullest day. It eliminates boredom from our lives.

CHRISTOPHER ISHERWOOD/SWAMI PRABHAVANANDA

Well-makers lead the water wherever they like; fletchers bend the arrow; carpenters bend a log of wood; wise people fashion themselves.

TEACHINGS OF THE BUDDHA

Chapter 9

INNER ALCHEMY

It is extremely necessary to pay attention to transformation now, while you are still in your pink scuba suit. Rather than transformation, let us call it transmutation. Not just change or growth, but alchemy.

In the Middle Ages, alchemy was the transmutation of "vile metal into gold." Lead, the ductile, opaque metal, was mainly used through the centuries to hold things down, from fishermen's nets to boat keels. Gold, the untarnishable "solar" metal, was the eternal prize and goal. You might think this alchemy is a poetic metaphor. Let me tell you something rather astounding: In physics, the atomic formation of gold differs from that of lead by only one particle in orbit. If one could knock it off orbit, out of the previous formation, the transmutation could be physically realized. Of course we can do it in our modern cyclotrons, but the cost is more than the benefit. The beauty of it is that it was known by Arabian alchemists before the first year of our calendar!

But the main goal of the serious alchemist was the transmutation of the alchemist himself. And this is our job. As we are, there is too much lead in our molecular "soul" and very little gold indeed.

What is all this lead that holds us down? It's as though we try to fly, but we're still holding on tight to our heavy baggage. Picture yourself trying to take off and soar, while in each hand you hold a suitcase filled with cement. Our baggage consists of defects, conditioning—conditioning reinforced by endless feedback—programming, attachments, concepts, and all the mental infrastructure. The real difficulty is that this baggage is not separate from us, like so many suitcases; it's part of us. How can we rid ourselves of this old baggage? Let's start with the defects.

Unraveling the Knots

The Buddhist tradition refers to anger, greed, laziness, jealousy, and so on as "negative aggregates." These are built-up habits that form a sort of knot. All these knots create something we might think of as a hand-knit sweater. You begin by picking your largest knot of built-up habit and unravel it. A big knot will take about three months. A really big knot, such as alcoholism or drug addiction, will take longer. Pretty soon, knot by knot, the sweater will begin to unravel—because once you are able to get rid of one knot, the others are weakened.

Even small "technical errors" are important. Procrastination, for example. It is more a weakness than an addiction, but it is a dangerous trend, and definitely a part of the heavy negative netting that holds us down.

The Jigsaw Puzzle

This technique for eliminating defects is called the Jigsaw Puzzle. First of all, imagine yourself as you are in the negative state. Perhaps choose to work on anger. In the mirror, try to see exactly how you look when you are angry—jaw clenched, eyes wide or narrow.

Now see this picture clearly on your mindscreen, but *without emotion or judgment*. See that image as a jigsaw puzzle, with thin lines indicating the different pieces. You shake it and it breaks up, as though sucked out through an airplane window into the night. The pieces fly in all directions, turning over and over, catching starlight. You are left with only the star-filled night sky, the serenity of infinite space. Feel that serenity. And *cut*: end of technique.

If the negative aggregate you wish to rid yourself of is difficult to visualize, work with it until you finally can come up with a vivid picture that represents that defect.

You do not need to do the Jigsaw in meditation, you can do it any time when you can bring your attention to the details. But do it faithfully every day until you realize the defect is gone. It is the first technique I give to new students, and hundreds have testified over the years that it really works.

Creating Yourself as a Higher Being

You have already learned about the three vehicles. The sum of their characteristics forms our personality, and it is just as fluid, impermanent, and unreal as our three vehicles. It is extremely sensitive to criticism and, as you know, it just loves flattery. It is small, puny, and easily damaged in this world of unpredictability.

When we start to free ourselves of this personality, as we climb up the mountain of wisdom, it's like leaving dear friends while we take an outside elevator to a higher floor. They're waving to us, but they're much smaller. By the time we get to the top, they're almost invisible. Perhaps we can communicate as though by telephone, and they will give us their reactions. We can give them instructions because we can see what they should do—we have a great view from up there.

People perceive us quite differently than we perceive ourselves. Since we create ourselves, why not create ourselves as higher beings? Begin by de-dramatizing—if you take yourself seriously, you condense yourself at the level of the opinion of others. You acquire power in exact relation to the bettering of your qualities. Manifest yourself *fully* and there will be happiness.

Remember, we are what we create, dead or alive. If you say this life is nothing but a tough, violent jungle, you make your own world of props, creating the patterns of your life. You are creating a hell, living at a lower vibration.

We must look at ourselves without all the projections of the vehicles. It's like a house of mirrors: Simultaneously, you are each distorted image. But you can only see them one at a time.

First, take a good look at your physical self. Look carefully in the mirror. Say to yourself, "I am not that. I am not the pink covering called skin. I am not the grinding teeth. I am not the little eyes. I am not this scuba suit of a body. I am not this bionic machine. I simply live in it."

Next consider the astral body of emotions. The frantic monkey cage. "No, I am not that."

Then the mind. "Am I my mind?" It is never calm, always chattering, always responding to emotions. I can watch it do so. "Am I my thoughts?" I can see that my thoughts have been put together by all the trash in the world. "No, I am not that."

Now watch other people in this same detached way, as though you were an extraterrestrial visitor, curious about Earthlings and how they function. See the other people as bionic machines. Go to a shopping mall, a restaurant. Imagine that you slip out backwards from your body, stand still and watch. Tell yourself: I am awake. I am aware. You will notice a change. The other people seem to be in a dream state. They are like ghosts, projected. See the beings in their bionic machines – the latex-like skin covering, the small darting eyes which take in so little, the hair which covers the fragile parts. See what they are made of. In a restaurant watch how they stuff their mouths. See how their muscles pull their faces according to their emotions. See their clothes as coverings.

This is not a pleasant technique. You are not seeing beauty. It is a cold vision. If you try it when you are having sex, it will most definitely kill desire. But try it for a week. Because through this exercise you will gain the *evidence* that you are not your vehicle. And this is another step forward in your transmutation, your alchemy.

Superstition

We are attached to our belief in "reality" here, to concepts, to fears of illness, bombs, earthquakes. We are in a cage made of these fears. Most of the things we're afraid of never happen, but they poison our life. We hold ourselves down and then wonder why we can't fly! Break the limitations which *you yourself* create every day.

We need to free ourselves of the concept of being a *unique* reality. We think our problems are real because we live in a real world. It's not. There are other worlds just as real, just as relative. For example, the microscopic one—the millions and millions of cells in our own body. On a slightly larger scale, there are minute creatures that look a bit like lobsters and who make a living in our eyelashes. There are some in our scalps. Think of all the tiny creatures who exist in a drop of water. Train a microscope on a piece of cheese: It's a zoo, teeming with life!

Superstition is part of our heavy baggage. We often see ourselves through the eyes of a lot of dead fools. Watch out for feedback such as "You are not worthy." Fight this feeling. Dissolve it. It is a lot of religious bosh. If you did something wrong it was through ignorance. Now you are on the path of wisdom, and you are working on self-transformation. Then, when you feel you are beyond the activity around you, and that you are looking for something more, don't put yourself down for feeling that way. It means you are maturing, that you are on your quest. Your empowerment is at hand.

For a week, try this exercise: *Don't accept anything.* Question your opinions on what is, even if you've had them since childhood. Question what you were taught in school, from first grade on. The beliefs we are rooted in give us feedback and prevent us from changing. We need to make changes without creating feedback.

It's better not to have a "belief system." A "working hypothesis" is better. After all, don't forget everything is real on its level of reality.

When at last we get rid of the lies that sustain us, then there is nothing. Then we have to take on ourselves the responsibility of action—with no rules to go by, with no created Divinity as obstacle. Then we are ready for the quantum leap.

So, reduce everything to its *essence.* All life is a field of energy within other fields of energy at different grades of cohesion. If you reduce something to its essence, there are no contradictions. Reduce all problems to the common denominator.

This can make a good theme for a meditation: We, human beings, are different cohesions of energy. And energy is forever.

Another meditation: We are just pure energy. The world around us is just pure energy. So everything is possible. The world is in our brain, through our translation. It is not "out there." Will this world end when the last eye closes? Sure—but don't forget it really never existed.

We need to do a lot of cleansing. I have often called my school "a big washing machine." Naturally, we need to cleanse away our negative defects. But it is just as important to cleanse the deep-rooted superstitions, concepts, and belief systems.

Nonattachment

The teachings of Buddha counsel detachment. This does not mean detachment from close ties, such as child, parent, or spouse. Nonattachment should never take the form of indifference to those who are in need of your love and service. It should instead be indifference to the material wants and desires of your existence, the constant striving to seek pleasure and avoid pain.

Try to separate your needs from your wants. You will see that they are not necessarily the same. Examine: are your needs on the same level as your desires? Examine, speculate, unfold, shuffle. This will lead you to: "What am I made of? What part is real?"

Hand in hand with attachment come expectations, which are very built-in and cause us no end of trouble. When we want people to fit our models, our expectations, we are bound to be frustrated. This is why so many marriages fail. If each partner would only leave all expectations outside, before crossing the threshold, the divorce rate would plummet.

The trick of nonattachment is to be involved in what you do, but aware that you are involved. Then you will not be attached. Practice a serene acceptance. Be aware, and work, love, and live with detached awareness.

Conditioning

Part of the alchemical work to be done on ourselves is the creation of new brain circuitry. This will definitely accelerate your evolution. Get into the great unused part of your brain and learn to use it to relate to the cosmos. What you are not conscious of does not exist for you. Remember, the expansion of consciousness is the capacity to have more relations with everything. You must expand spherically, like a balloon, not in a linear or lopsided way. If you can envision a multidimensional existence, your development will be in a thousand directions.

Again, think of the brain as a radio. It perceives, transmutes, emits. Push your circuits to multiply. Stimulate them. Experiment.

Logic is inferior to intuition. You know by now that logic is mechanical, put together like a game for kids—the pieces (syllogisms) are bound to fit together. Instead, try to understand through *analogies*. An approximate understanding will cause the brain circuits to awaken. Dormant circuits awaken by the association of ideas. Heat up those circuits from below. Wake them up. You can do it—already we use more circuits than people who lived a few thousand years ago.

We must also be able to understand much better than we do the *conditioning* of our vehicles. This is the theory of conditioned automatism, also called automatic reflexes. For instance, if I tell you that I will cut a lime in half and squeeze a few drops on your tongue, you will automatically salivate, whether I am holding a real lime or none at all. Your mental image will be quite sufficient to trigger the production of saliva.

Since this was demonstrated by Pavlov in Russia around the end of the last century, we have discovered that the whole activity of our metabolism, and that of animals, is the result of multiple chain reactions of conditioned reflexes which grew parallel to the physiological complexity of each species. This is understandable in our physical system, but it is also reproduced in our mental and emotional worlds.

You see, we are all a sort of summit of a genealogical pyramid.

Looking down we see father and mother, grandpa and grandma, great grandparents, and so on and on until, whether we have kept track of it or not, we know there is a cave-couple who started the chain. All those ancestors of ours laughed and cried, loved and fought, were born, lived, and died, accumulating during their existence a myriad of attractions and repulsions, renewing and repeating an infinity of habits, choices, and acts, which finally automatized in their emotional bodies.

These we have inherited. We have them in our genes and chromosomes, buried in our deepest subconscious levels. Those who are not *aware* go through life thinking they are choosing or refusing, while in fact they have been totally conditioned by these subterranean currents. They feel each choice as their choice, their individual decision, spontaneous and openly taken; they come to believe finally that they have "free will" to decide and act.

Free Will

The free will question has always constituted a theological stumbling block. The churches have had extremely capable philosophical minds to serve their goal of expansion. Please do not take "expansion" to mean colonialism. Expansion of faith (Christian, Moslem, Hindu, or whatever) was considered by sincere religious leaders as the only goal in life. They were so worried about the salvation of *their* souls, that they could only feel comfortable if everybody else would join them on their bandwagon. The less opposition, the more objectivity to their truth. And so, by a strange phenomenon of collective hypnosis, they finally ended up taking for an evident fact the complex little stories they had personally made up. (This is, of course, a parenthesis, and throws no shadow on the great consciousnesses like Christ or Buddha. We are speaking here of the organizers and public relations specialists.)

The problem of free will is simple: Do we have it or don't we?

Suppose we haven't. As the Moslems say, "It is written." In

which case, why worry? Whatever you do, one way or another, won't change your lines in the script.

On the other hand, if we do have it, we have to admit that our so-called free will really isn't. Because things we "will" to happen very often just don't.

So, back to our theologists. They found a way to wriggle out of the difficulty. They said God gave human beings the choice between good and evil. And in order to avoid confusion—because what is evil for me may be great for you—they pointed to their particular book with its set of rules: you comply, you go to heaven; you don't, you go down to the grillroom, and that's all, folks!

Well, at the beginning, this worked wonders with simple people, but I'm afraid it won't satisfy my readers. Let's give the free will question a more serious look. At the front of this book is a phrase at once very simple and very deep, that Seneca said centuries ago: "The willing, Destiny guides them; the unwilling, Destiny drags them."

(Seneca was a very wise Roman who had the misfortune to be the mentor of a rather unpleasant pupil—the Emperor Nero. The pupil was in his twenties, and after his fifth year of a reasonable reign he developed awful manias and vices. He had, of course, inherited some from his mother—whom he poisoned, by the way, during one of his juvenile tantrums. Seneca, who was a bit old-fashioned, disapproved of this kind of behavior, so Nero ordered him to commit suicide. Which Seneca did. I suppose that at his age living in the Roman orgy set had become boring. There is a tender note, though. Seneca's lady friend, a liberated slave, refused to leave him, and opened her veins with him in the same bath.)

Back to Seneca's phrase. If we are of the "willing" he talks about, do we have this free will we are trying to define? What is this destiny which is supposed to guide us? Or drag us?

As usual, these big questions are resolved by a greater synthesis. To the thesis "we have free will" and its antithesis that "we do not," we have the greater synthesis which absorbs both. We see the cosmic Will manifested so clearly, so evidently, in all natural phenomena. Every blade of grass, every living being, from the visible manifestation of its life to the most fundamental thrust for growth, craves liberty. And this craving for liberty ranges from a conscious need to an instinctive hope of liberation from *form*—that is, the return after eons of manifestation to the primordial essence, the world's prenatal state, the closing of the cycle of existence after all lessons are learned and all powers acquired.

We find this yearning in all the traditions—the "return to the Father," the nostalgia we feel when we contemplate the starlit sky. This powerful current toward the completion of all experience is the great cosmic Will, the "let Thy Will be done" of the prayer, the last words of the dying Buddha: "Exhausted is the fuel, extinguished the flame, this is the end of existence," and with a sigh of relief he added, "Nirvana," which he had already reached during his life, and into which he finally blended.

So, in practical application to our daily life, where finally all wisdom finds its touchstone, if we throw ourselves into collaboration with this current and "serve" this ever-present craving in all creatures, we shall then be carried by this force, guided by this destiny of the manifested. And then all the obstacles that bar the way of our fellow humans will serve us as building blocks for the construction of our stairway to heaven. We shall see to our surprise the resolution of all our problems, appearing to us like the thick layer of ice on a river, which the oncoming warmth of spring suddenly breaks up, the huge pieces dragged along by the growing current to vanish into the sea.

Remember, we are the creators of our world. By hitching our cart to the team of the gods, we are bound to end up winners.

Transmutation as a Becoming

Let me close this chapter on alchemy by explaining that your transmutation process is a *becoming*. It is becoming the higher levels of consciousness, covibrating with them. The higher levels mean greater light, therefore greater atomic speed or vibration. This goes perfectly well with modern physics, which will tell you that light is composed of waves and particles. Light, which is a synthesis of all its colors—dazzling white—is of extremely rapid vibration. At that level we receive through our sense channels hundreds of millions of particles per second. So for us, who are still in syntony with the cellular vibration of the physical level, the jump into molecular vibration, into the high levels of light, means a real, tremendous evolutionary *leap.* This is the quantum leap of which theoretical physicists speak, but which they cannot yet carry beyond the blackboard.

The axis for growth should be love, because at our human level love is the *only* thing that acts as light, the life-giving force. We can visualize our heart center with a dazzling white light, but how can we *realize*—make real—that light? The leap from one low level to the highest one is really "dying to be reborn," because as we die to all our old vibrations, which are the substance of all our attachments, we are reborn as a very high vibration. Then we are just as different from our present self as our present self is different from the little baby when it first appeared.

A Meditation on Becoming

The leap to Nirvana is itself a noneffort, a shedding, an abandoning, a throwing away, an undressing of the soul. It is a leap through the transmutation of elements. For that leap we need power, so now sit in meditation and reverence. Bring awareness to your heart *chakra* in the middle of your chest. See it/feel it as dazzling white energy. This primordial energy, known to the Hindus as *prana*, to the Chinese as *chi*, and to the quantum physicists as *the field*, will *only* follow a thought channel—so it will accumulate in our heart through our inner vision.

Now feel that light in your brain, at the third eye or pineal gland, deep between the brows. Fill your head with light and send it out through the crown, higher and higher. Feel that you are sending light from the energy you have brought up from the heart, from the dazzling white light at the heart chakra. This is your tie to the light of the higher levels with which you will covibrate, which you will *become*.

COMMUNICATING WITH THE COSMOS

Realize every event in the indefinite number of universes is influenced by you; realize there is life in everything; realize you are not what you've been taught; allow consciousness to unite with you.

BOB TOBEN

And this our life, exempt from public haunt,
Finds tongues in trees, books in the running brooks,
Sermons in stones, and good in everything.

WILLIAM SHAKESPEARE

The world is too much with us; late and soon,
Getting and spending, we lay waste our powers;
Little we see in Nature that is ours.

WILLIAM WORDSWORTH

There is nothing to be saved *from*, no struggle of life *against* the universe, no God outside the world to be feared and obeyed; only the Goddess, the Mother, the turning spiral that whirls us in and out of existence . . . whose laughter bubbles and courses through all things and who is found only through love: love of trees, of stones, of sky and clouds, of scented blossoms and thundering waves; of all that runs and flies and swims and crawls on her face; through love of ourselves . . .

STARHAWK

For everyone hath all things in himself, and again sees all things in another, so that all things are everywhere and all is all and each is all, the glory is infinite.

PLOTINUS

Chapter 10

COMMUNICATING WITH THE COSMOS

Now that you are walking the path of wisdom, and you have been given the definition of godhood, you are aware that you need to relate more and more to the rest of the cosmos. It is time for you to create rapport with all the beings, visible and invisible, in your world.

Telepathy

Too often the human experiences a feeling of lonely isolation from others. It is the bulwark of our senses, our "bubble," which gives us the impression of being separated, as we each, through our senses, create our own world. Even two lovers feel separated, always wanting to be closer—the sexual act itself is a copenetration—they feel they can never be close enough.

In our feeling of isolation we try to communicate to each other. But we use words.

What does "I love you" mean exactly? Depends on who says it. It could mean marriage at the altar, or the motel next door. What is a word? If I say, "I'll give you an apple," what apple? There are millions of apples. We need to be precise with words. We always have to embroider with details, especially with emotion, until we finally focus on something we consider complete.

But there is a way to communicate without words, a silent,

unspoken way, which puts an end to the feeling of lonely isolation. Some people call it telepathy—thought transmission, but it really isn't that. What is transmitted is a state of consciousness, which like all feelings is immediately brought to the brain. It really is a deep identity of tone.

What telepaths do we know?

All babies are telepaths until about age two. Watch a baby look into the eyes of a new person. The baby will receive the inner value of that person. If the baby smiles, okay. If the baby cries and runs away, beware: There's something there that the infant consciousness receives as a wallop, as an impact. Dogs are also telepaths, and cats are, wonderfully—they keep their distance until they've received all the information about you. Then, only if you are okay will they come and rub themselves against you. In fact, all animals and insects are telepathic.

We humans have the capacity to develop telepathy. Only our attitude makes it difficult for us. We are used to our noisy communication system. Unfortunately, inner silence, which in telepathy or consonance is obviously a must, is not the average person's cup of tea. So, once we've brought together all the data fed in by our senses, which are constantly receiving and asking for decisions about our reaction to the sensory impact; coupled with the mania we have for announcing our ideas and making them predominant over the thoughts and feelings of others; and added the flow of mnemonic images and brain chatter, it's not surprising that we can hardly "feel" the telepathic message and its mental translation. Through inner silence and training, however, we can definitely achieve it.

Remember, telepathy is the receiving of an astral impact. This creates a sensation, and all sensations are translated on the mind-screen as *images*. When I say that a human cannot think without images, I do not mean that the image must be visual. There are auditory images, there are olfactory images, there are taste images. For instance, if you pick up a piece of apple pie in the kitchen and eat it *without looking at it*, it appears clearly and vividly as if on a color poster as what it is, apple pie. A certain fragrance you have smelled in the past can immediately bring to mind a whole landscape. A song first heard when you were in love will do the same—it will bring back the place, the dancing, the feeling. We always end up with something that our consciousness can understand and our mind can perceive, in order to know how to act.

Because telepathy is received astrally, it is sometimes difficult to transmit something as abstract as numbers. But numbers can have a qualitative value for us. For example, one may seem serene; four square, or solid, and so on. The ace of spades has a different impact than the ace of hearts—it is a bad omen, for some. But the poor card itself has nothing to do with it.

Mothers of soldiers at war often feel the impact when their sons are injured or killed. But why would a woman feel this impact as flames, say, when her son died in a shipwreck? Because the astral message was translated by symbols in *her* memory bank. For her, the ultimate horror was flames.

Opening Up to Other Consciousnesses

What is important on your fast-forward path to wisdom is to open up to other consciousnesses. First of all, I suggest you learn how to make contact with the whole world of Nature, where the telepathic capacity exists. Most human beings still suffer from the pseudoscientific arrogance of the last few centuries, believing that life belongs only to what we can, with our five drastically limited senses, perceive as appearing to be alive. But *everything* on our planet is animated by life, and where there is life there is a form of consciousness.

For example, very few people know what trees really are. They'll say, "Oh sure, wood and leaves. Oaks and such. Nice, gives shade." Or they'll see it commercially—so many feet of lumber, so much width, costs so much. This is a little bit like looking at trees as the military brass looks at soldiers: as units—often dispensable, alas.

You see, I have to remind you again, we have focused all our life on Reason. It has no emotions—a computer will give you the news that your mother died with the same indifference as the news that the soup is ready. It doesn't care. It cannot—it hasn't the capability. Once Reason has produced the image of the news, the whole astral body swings into an upsurge of emotions, and the heart is "broken." Reason has already retired, as it cannot participate in any emotion.

But we have overdeveloped it. Near the end of 1790, during the French Revolution, the Committee of Public Safety fired God and passed the job on to Reason, calling her (in French, Reason is of the feminine gender) the Goddess Reason, and honoring her with a national holiday! Unfortunately, this sort of overemphasis has brought our world to the point of catastrophe.

Good old Reason, cold and logical. We nearly kill all the whales. Why? Because of money. Money buys possessions, therefore kill the whales! It's the same with the underground nuclear test explosions. People will shrug and say, "So what? It makes a cavern. Why worry about some rocks?" Well, wait and see.

Even the hardest rocks are alive. They are consciousnesses, although one second of their dynamics, sustained by an incredible atomic activity, would translate on our level of perception as a hundred thousand years. They are part of our Mother Earth. What will be the effect of such explosions? We don't know. Because we only live on the surface of our mind. All the other dimensions are absolutely unknown to us.

How can we develop a sense of union, a syntony—identity of tone—with other beings? With humans, it is extremely difficult. The human personality has been built up over the years. Humans attack before being attacked, because they know it's the best defense. They pretend, they masquerade, they deceive even themselves to appear as they want. So humans are a tough nut to crack—unless you have developed the capacity to enter into deep reverential states without any emotions, without any personality, capable of loving beings for what they are worth and what their essence is (which they do not yet know). If you can come to that level, then you can see right through human beings and they look as if they were drawn on a pane of glass.

The Divine Love of the Sun

Let us look for just one moment at the sun. Like everything else in our cosmos it has life, but on such a vast scale we can scarcely conceive it. Our sun is a sidereal entity, a star; from its light a whole system of planets functions and lives, and on the planets are beings visible or invisible.

The sun sends out an extraordinary power that gives life to everything on our planet. When there is sunlight, everything grows. Now, what is this light? Light does not exist as we think it does. We and the animals and insects around us are the only ones that have combined their cells in order to make a little machine that reacts to light—the eyes. But if there were no eyes, we would still feel the heat. What is that? Science will tell you it is photons of light. But that doesn't explain it.

What is this projection from the sun, this throw of life-giving energy? It is divine love. Divine, because it is not human—clearly beyond humanity. The sun is a colossal, powerful being. Nothing else spreads life on this earth and through its call lifts everything, vertically, towards its source of light, life and power.

St. Francis, in his great simplicity, sent his reverent love to Brother Sun and Sister Moon. The Native Americans, with the same reverence, speak of Grandfather Sun and Grandmother Earth. We can all learn from these traditions.

Sending Love to Animals, Insects, and Plants

Let us start by entering souls which do not attack, which do not pretend, those who are open to cosmic, impersonal love. When we want to communicate without using words and constructing sentences, or bothering with machines like typewriters, we should remember the way a mother communicates with her child. When the child is a year old she doesn't explain things—she says words that are states of consciousness for her that the child understands beautifully, as a dog does. You can talk absolute mumbo-jumbo for half an hour and the dog will listen with the greatest attention, absorbing your love through your voice.

Some animals have interests that are so different from ours that we don't know what to communicate. But we can always send love. Take, for instance, a big fish. Jacques Cousteau goes under the sea and he scratches the head of a fish. He's such a loving being to all these entities that they come and get warmed by his love. They bask in it.

The sun gives light to everything, and its power is cosmic impersonal love. We, through the heart *chakra*, are capable of producing and transmitting the same phenomenon.

But we have to focus upon the interest of the one we're talking to. If you try to explain philosophy to three year olds, they'll soon get bored and go away. But tell them a fairy tale and they'll sit in rapt attention. So if you deal with beings that are not human, think for a few minutes: Now what is this little brother of mine feeling, seeing, hearing? How does it see my world?

Let's take bees, for instance. I have a great friendship with bees, which are solar creatures. If you are afraid, a bee might hurt you, for fear is contagious. With love, never—for love is peace. I will often fish a bee out of the pool with my hand. I help the bee to dry, I tell it in which direction to fly, where to find flowers. Bees understand geometry. Every morning before taking off for the harvest, they do a geometrical dance on the sill of their hives.

You can also create a friendship with flies. They love to play. When a fly alights on your hand, look to see if it is a young fly—size will indicate that. Then don't slap, don't hit—forget our stupid human violence. Pretend you want to hit the fly with your finger, playfully, slowly. The fly will take off, then immediately come back, and always on the same place. This will go on for a few minutes. You will see it's a game—you are playing with a "puppy" fly, and a feeling you have never had will fill your heart.

Then the fly will tire of it and leave you, or it may find you and start the game all over.

Leave a fly swatter on the table—they know what it's for. How can they know? Mother flies cannot teach their young ones like a mammal does, they lay their eggs and fly off. Still, the insect group soul knows. Being aware that flies have intelligence makes us more reverent. If a fly is bothering you, address the group soul with reverence and affection: "Mother Fly, please tell your children to leave me alone for half an hour." Try it. Remember, never believe what I say, always experiment for yourself.

Now let us extend into the world of plants. The plant world is a state of consciousness which we perceive in certain condensations of shape and form. Wild and domestic plants (which are like house pets) all have life, and grow. They communicate and help each other. One may extend a branch to give shade to another that would burn, I have seen it happen many times.

Yet we think plants are immobile. We relegate the plants to an inferior position because of their incapacity to move from one place to another. For us humans, forced immobility appears as the most horrifying curse. In fact, any time we want to punish people, the first and most drastic way to do so is to reduce their living space, put them in jail.

Like every living being we perceive on earth, plants are composed of a condensed body (the one we see); a molecular (astral) body pervading its cells; and is also endowed with an instinctive—and to a certain degree autonomous—intelligence. In addition, there is an electronic intelligence element which belongs more to the mother soul of the species than to the particular plant itself. The plant's astral body is very well developed, and can be seen in Kirlian photography (in which the subtle energy of a body is recorded on photographic film). Like ours, it responds through syntony, or covibration if you prefer, to any emotional situation arising in the astral. This state of sensitivity is very like that of humans and animals, each according to its psychic development.

The plant's electronic body is of an angelic nature. Through the centuries these entities have been given various names—angels, *devas*, elementals, according to place and tradition. I think this needs to be better explained. All the traditional cultures, through the experience of living more intimately with natural phenomena, realized that in this world everything is hierarchic, from the little worm to the philosopher and beyond. They understood clearly that man and woman were far from being the top of the evolutionary scale. Humanity itself offered a clear vision of this graduation: from primitive brutes interested only in satisfying their physiological needs, to the most developed human beings capable of sacrificing these needs for the well-being of their brothers and sisters.

Therefore, in the hierarchy of consciousnesses we find some beings of high frequencies; these are traditionally called *devas* in India. Then there are others of lower vibrations called elementals of Nature; and some frankly much lower (as the elementals of belladonna, tobacco, and the *cannabis indica*) which belong to the middle and low astral planes.

Some plants are very soothing to us because an angelic elemental is there. Each plant manifests itself according to the nature of its *deva*.

A tree either grows from a seed or is transplanted. Now that being, when a seed, starts with a little sprout—generally white, transparent, extremely vulnerable. Nevertheless, it is surrounded by the love of earth forces—the entities of earth—which have no shape, but for centuries and in all parts of the world have been illustrated by artists and poets as little old men with long beards. These "gnomes" help the tree survive the hard process of birth. They take care to direct this little sprout so that its head is not stuck against stones, but comes out finally to the sun. At that moment it is not the gnomes' business any more. From then on the elemental of the plant takes over—very much like the human child, when the astral and etheric bodies begin to interact and function.

Like a nurse, the elemental of that tree will now help it grow, will do its best to influence the thought forms of the bugs around it. That tree extends its roots, builds its body up from the earth, taking the mineral salts, just like we do. It is a prayer, from the beginning of its appearance—little "hands" out, which we call leaves and branches—and is there, receiving life from the sun, the great consciousness who transmutes the love of the cosmos into life-giving energy. In this loving light the tree grows in a constant prayer.

The scientists will tell you the tree needs the sun for photosynthesis. I know. So what? Yes, it needs to create the photosynthesis for its body. But how did it ever come to that point? What is there within the tree? The scientists will not know, because they don't yet have instruments sensitive to the highly subtle causes, they can only measure the effects. As the great botanist, Chandra Bose, said: "If you want to know about a tree, you must become a tree."

From such a pragmatic teacher as I am, these descriptions of Nature might sound like a child's cartoon, or seem too sentimental and unscientific. I have talked to you about the latest quantum physics, and here I am speaking of gnomes and the sun's light as love! However, by now you are surely capable of looking at everything in your world with a fresh vision. If you have followed along and tested for yourself these explanations and techniques, you know that things are definitely not always what they seem, and I hope that after you finish this book, you will accept nothing until you have the evidence for yourself. All I can do is point the way, and offer some methods for your experiments.

Back to our tree. When it is grown strong, it starts exercising. It sways with the winds and builds its muscles, which are all the rings visible inside the trunk, added for every year of life. It opens up as a service for the other life forms that come to live in its branches. The tree's attention is up there, where it is the father, and worries hardly at all about its roots any more.

At the same time the tree transforms its sensitivity as an antenna. Why an antenna? Because we live in a closed circle of air, in layers of atmosphere, stratosphere, ionosphere, each one less dense. Mother Earth doesn't let molecules of air escape—it's all held together. So inside that belt of air which covers the earth, are all the emissions of the world's thought forms, the emotions, everything. And it goes around the planet. Everyone has noticed that inventions, when they appear, generally do so on several continents at the same time—because there are no barriers in a medium that functions through affinity and syntony.

All the thought forms produced with certain precision and energy remain for a short time as imprints in the astral of the atmosphere itself. A thought form, being of an electronic density, defines or sculpts the denser astral medium, which is molecular, and is then perceived by the elementals of the trees. This creates the memory capital of the older trees, which we humans can tap into.

This also presents to you the great unity of the cosmos, where every living being is (although unknowingly) bound to every living form. To meditate seriously on this can solve many a moral problem as well as explain what seems to be the injustice of our destiny.

Talking to the Trees

From the closed system of air, the trees fill themselves with a wisdom which is not egoistic. When you want to communicate with one of these wise beings, the first thing to do is go to a place where the trees have not clammed up because of the noise and stink of the city. Go to a big garden, or out in the country. If you are in California, try to visit the redwoods. Some have been alive more than three thousand years. Think of what they know! Choose a forest anywhere. The world is full of beautiful trees—let yourself be guided by your attraction.

The best time to communicate is at sunset, when the activity of these interacting worlds is nearer to rest. All day long the trees are busy, like you and me. At sunset, when the shadows of the trees are stretching, our own sensitivity expands. The elemental of the tree also has a tendency to stretch out at night, and relate with the forest around him. If you are a woman, you can receive a lot of love from the tree, and from the entities that are in between the trees and the bushes. The ancients used to speak of the fauns, the nymphs, the elves, and so on. These are names for consciousnesses of nature. Most are *yang* (male polarity), fewer are *yin* (female polarity). Trees, which are *yang*, do give out love; they are extremely attracted by feminine sensitivity, which is *yin*.

Put your back against the tree and sit down in any position you want, as long as your back is well against the tree. First calm your heartbeats, your chattering brain, your emotions. Let your physical body relax totally, until you have absolutely forgotten it. Then, with your mind and body at rest, imagine yourself embracing the trunk and send your loving thoughts to the wise being towering above you.

Be reverential. Use no personalisms. Just send out love, an impersonal sentiment that goes beyond standards of beauty—a reverential, far-reaching cosmic love for all the manifestations on the planet. This is a state of consciousness without which no high extrasensory contacts can ever be established. *It is the key that opens the souls of all beings, visible and invisible.* The lives around us can only notice ours if there is a bridge, or common spiritual denominator between us. And that is reverential love. It must be sincere—it cannot be faked.

After a minute, the tree will notice that a being full of love and respect is there at its foot. His awareness is never down there, it's always up high because of the big family of life forms in the branches. So the tree will be joyfully surprised to find that an evolved human consciousness is trying communication.

It's rather like when your dog puts a paw or its nose on your foot. You might be reading an important document, and suddenly you feel that one of your feet is hot, so you bring your attention down and you see the dog there. This is what the tree does—it suddenly feels a warm spot of love. And the tree's awareness will come down. My friends, you cannot imagine the joy and the warmth and protection that will surround you—this wise being has centuries behind it. Now you can just bask in that love. Send it and get it back. Stay in peaceful but acute awareness.

If you feel like it, ask the tree a question you have been trying to solve. It will answer immediately—not with words, but exactly, with a wave of evidential teaching. You will receive it suddenly and completely, as if you had just remembered a long-forgotten fact. You see, motionless plants, so helpless on our level, are very powerful actors on the astral plane. Remember that on the astral plane, events are gestated before they ever get to our 3-D level. To put it succinctly: The tree taps into all the wisdom vibrating on that plane, you tap into the tree. But only by using that bridge of love.

You will only have to experience this communion once to realize you have opened a door to unlimited expansion of consciousness. This first experience is such an awe-inspiring reality that it will dwarf in your mind all the analytical forms of knowledge that normal humans believe to be the ne plus ultra of recognition. Understand that it is a step similar to that of a man, blind since birth, who is suddenly able to see and receive the impact of our multicolored world.

It would be an error to think of this as some sort of codified message through a language or imagery. This order of communication is quite different—it is *becoming* the answer to our question, absorbing it instantaneously into our individuality. In other words, we grow into the answer, and become mature through the fact. It is a spontaneous expansion.

If you do these exercises seriously, as often as you can, you will begin to develop telepathy with beings who offer no screens. It goes right through. And remember that our Mother Earth is programmed for diversity—different trees have different states of consciousness and different elementals.

The magnolia is the body of a very ancient elemental, or soul. Magnolia trees were here before the appearance of the first dinosaurs, or at least simultaneously with them—around 400 million years ago. How much can a consciousness accumulate of wisdom to be able to survive 400 million years and flourish as a beautiful tree? Most of the plants of that age have vanished, or dwindled in size. So this tree is a wonder. Sit with it in reverence and humility. What can we learn that this magnificent being must know? We don't have to have a computer inside our head to be able to understand, to be able to communicate.

This is a chance for you to communicate with other levels, other dimensions. A man needs a lot of love, reverence, and humility to do this. Go around sunset, when the trees' elementals are starting to breathe and come out. If you go with the usual arrogance of this killer race, then they clam up totally and you get no contacts. For a man, it is easier to connect with small running brooks, which have *yin* energy and are full of female, *yin* creatures—the entities of water. Go by the water, stop thinking, and receive those wavelengths. Just feel as if you were listening to a group of young girls laughing and chatting. You will then turn the attention of the water sprites toward you, and listening to the babbling of the brook as it runs on the stones and moss you will learn the mysteries of womanhood.

A man who goes deep into the woods at night will feel apprehensive. He may start whistling to keep up courage. He will feel he is in a place not sympathetic to him. Because all these forest entities are very masculine, very *yang*, they and the man will repel like two positive magnets. But a woman will feel so much love that the experience becomes erotic. It's quite remarkable. The forest elementals don't care what a woman looks like; it is the feminine pulsation that they come to. They get a lot from it, and they give a lot.

Communicating with Other Plants

Each species has its own characteristics. Pine trees are solemn, Saturnian beings, quiet and puritanic. They have been around since before and during the dinosaurs, and witnessed the birth of Homo sapiens. Their shape has hardly changed. The spirit of a living being that is so unfailingly mature is a receptacle of infinite wisdom.

The orange tree is a joyous entity, associated with pleasure, and highly related to monetary affairs. Let's not forget that money is but a conventional symbol for energy exchange, which gives us joy, security, and often sincere happiness—therefore, pleasure.

One of the most powerful elementals that interacts with us humans belongs to the datura plant, which can grow into a big tree. The datura can literally explode in blossoming flowers when an intimate and magical relation is established between the human and itself.

The white laurel and the white rose have a very high angelic element. The white rose is a living symbol of the cosmic mother, the divine female principle, and participates intensely in the joys of a household. I have seen a white rosebush come up with three roses in full winter, the plant surrounded with snow, celebrating with this effort the birth of a long-awaited and hoped-for child.

The red rose is the same, but at an incarnate level—human maternity, female passion. The white rose can lift the human state of consciousness, the red rose can heal the human heart "broken" in a love affair. We humans suffer more from emotional traumas than physical illnesses during our lifetime, and many of our sorrows can be alleviated through the friendly effort of a compassionate elemental if we know the steps to take.

The double tuberose is an extraordinary flower, with its strong, sweet night fragrance. If you know the right technique, its gentle entity can provide a bridge into the astral world if you wish to travel to visit loved ones departed from this plane.

Through love and respect, ordinary houseplants can become like pets. If sincerely praised for their beauty, they will do their best to remain so. As they are extremely sensitive to praise, they also are extremely suspicious of visitors; and if you have ever sat and waited for someone in a room full of healthy plants, you might have picked up a feeling of silent watchfulness, as the plants focused their attention and suspicion on the quality of your thoughts and emotions.

Over the months and years, houseplants absorb our astral vibrations and those of our family. If they have been taken care of, with love and attention given to their needs, they will make great efforts to process our vibrations through theirs before giving them out again. Just as they give us oxygen, which we use to breathe and therefore energize our home atmosphere, they also energize and purify our vibrations. They try to balance our astral output, as they thrive on serenity and love, and wither away in an emotional atmosphere of hate and violence. Any emotional outburst makes them cringe in fear of destruction.

As we take care of them they develop dependence and confidence in us. You can caress a plant by stroking it one inch above its leaves—that's as far as its aura reaches. Talk to it as you would to a puppy. "You're so nice, you look beautiful today, let me clean the dust from your leaves. Thank you for keeping me company."

In a month's time the plant will move to you. This is hard work for the plant, as it must create elongated cells to stretch. Don't move it, just watch it extend in your direction. Some leaves and branches will go for the light, but one branch will come towards you. Because as you give love, it is equivalent to the light it gets from the window.

Light is love. This exercise with the plant will be your *evidence.*

Once I had a plant which was in a window, and I put next to it a small, bronze Hindu sculpture of a bodhisattva which had been worshiped in India. It left some of its branches to face and receive nourishment from light, and sent two branches toward the statue—curling around it, without using it as a support. That statue was saturated with reverence through centuries of devotion (metal conserves energy), and emitted on the invisible spectrum the identical love and life force that plants are always attracted to, that is, light.

Cosmic Ecology

Silent communication, remember, is all beyond Reason. We must not expect Reason to solve problems which do *not* pertain to the realm of the senses. When you tell Reason you're going to speak to a tree, Reason snaps: "What a fool. I don't believe this—you're completely nuts."

And rightly so. Reason can only think in terms of measuring the wood, the age, the height, and so forth. Our rational computer is inclined to think of Nature as "blind." There are no blind forces of Nature. Everything that is manifested, everything that is perceived, is composed of one or all of the four alchemical elements—earth, fire, water, air. And these compose our physical body, too. In our bones are minerals—that is, earth. We are made of water. We are, down to our smallest cells, heat and air. Therefore we *are* the elements. Now, everything that manifests itself is conscious of its life and manifestation. That is, everything has a conscious intelligence, cooperating in the task of the planet's metabolism. Because of our scale of observation, we call this ecology. The same elements cooperate in our reduced ecology, which we call metabolism. Therefore, through the principle of identity, *we are the cosmic consciousness*. And only our limited knowledge has deprived us of that awareness and evidence.

Remember that air, fire, water, and earth are the physical, perceivable bodies of the four elements, and that their intelligences, or souls, are never visible. This is why in ancient cultures, like that of the Greeks, the forces of Nature were illustrated and personalized as gods or powerful spirits. But our so-called pragmatic culture has reduced everything to abstract concepts and to chemical interactions which are the *effects*—the "how," but rarely the "why."

The recognition of the air in every cell of you makes you part of the air everywhere. It is an interchange. Air goes through you like the wind through the forest. Forget duality. Air is you; you are it. This will expand your consciousness, because it is not an intellectual affair. You don't have to imagine that you are air, fire, earth, or water. You are.

Water is an immense consciousness. It is everywhere. It is easy to feel ourselves as water—the saliva in the mouth, the blood in the veins, the liquid in the eyes. Like the air, the water around the earth is in a closed system, evaporates and condenses. Where is the division? You look at a fountain of water. You are a suit of skin with water in it, over there is a cement bowl with moving water in it. Only your limited Reason makes the separation. The whole thing is a unity. All the elements recycle, whether within our bodies or outside, recycle and interchange.

With air, it is even easier to understand, just breathe it in. Or feel one with the wind. You can feel it rushing through you — you become it. You are reverent, you are receptive, and everything clicks. It's an explosive state — there's gooseflesh. By the way, legendary Merlin's power was that he *was* everything.

So, if we *are* the elements, we are not isolated. Stop focusing on your individuality, and walk the world as consciousness. As the Native Americans say, "Walk the Earth in a sacred way." If you focus on your individuality, you're focusing on your limitations, your negative aggregates, your attachments and conditioning. Become part of the great Will which guides you to liberation from form.

We are surrounded by life — loving, open, wonderful life. And we must learn to communicate, because when you receive love and useful thought forms from other beings, you will see that you are not alone. The whole world is full of entities who are only waiting to communicate with you. And once you have made contact, just keep silent; there will be spontaneous revelations.

It is not difficult to understand that all the consciousnesses of the cosmos, except the lowest ones, do not suffer our problems. Most of our hatred, ambition, violence, and frustration, which constitute our astral and mental, do not exist in other more subtle life forms. Consciousnesses manifested on this 3-D level or below are the only ones who can be hungry, thirsty, too cold, or just too miserable. We are the only ones who are persuaded we are mortal and whose hearts are torn apart when our loved ones die. On other levels above ours, no one ever goes through this nightmare. That is why they are all anxious to help.

And now you know you are not alone, ever. Reach out in inner silence.

SERVICE AND COMPASSION

It is more blessed to give than to receive.

ACTS 20:35

The act of helping a suffering being ought to occur as spontaneously, as instinctively as the act of pulling back one hand quickly if it touches anything red-hot.

ALEXANDRA DAVID-NEEL

Try to serve truly. All power comes through true service.

SWAMI PARAMANANDA

The Inner Silence is self-surrender. And that is living without the sense of ego.

RAMANA MAHARSHI

As the blight of "noise-pollution" increasingly harasses our outer world, let us counteract it on the deepest level, by discovering that impenetrable stillness in our own being and radiating that peace to our fellow men.

GAYATRI DEVI

Chapter 11

SERVICE AND COMPASSION

At the highest level of hierarchy in the Catholic church is the pope. His title of Pontifex Maximus literally means the greatest bridge-maker. In other words, his work is to create an accessible passage from humans to their creator. On the other face of the honorific medal, the pope's other title is *Servus servorum dei,* or "servant of the servants of God." This is the most humble of all positions.

Whatever opinion one may have about organized religion, and whatever humanity has done with these teachings, one cannot avoid seeing some evident facts. After centuries the footprints of the great and strange messengers are still there, whether it be the Buddha or the Christ. It is evident these beings didn't come for profit. What profit has been obtained by the organizations built around their effort is another story, and doesn't concern me. But why did they come? What is the motive behind their striving to advise, guide, and alleviate human pain?

Service

The answer is very simple, perhaps too simple for most of us: service. To serve "an ailing humanity" which seems to go around in eternal circles of repeated failures. On the surface it seems that way and the historical evidence appears to back it up. But that misses the point: For the great consciousness that is taking this responsibility, the point of view is far above the historical horizon;

otherwise he would be immediately involved in it, and that would be politics.

The cynic would say, "Even so, why should anyone bother to serve a bunch of ferociously competitive primitives, these irritable apes who will tear you apart if you ever cross their path to success, possessions, and power?"

No one ever promised life would be easy. As soon as our young ones come out of the protective shell of school and home, in order to survive they must accept partial enslavement or enter the jungle. As Kipling poetically put it: "Good rest to all that keep the Jungle Law"—which, after all, is "eat or be eaten." And we know by experience that humans, even the dearest ones, are nice only as long as they don't bite. Indeed, as we live we finally wonder how we can justify, even to ourselves, any effort in the sense of "service," given the total indifference, aggressivity, and ingratitude of most humans.

Well, that's the view from the jungle floor. But through the process of inner growth we acquire another vision. The sequence of time changes. Time, this enemy of normal people with its feeling of opportunities slipping by, never to return (they never "knock twice," remember?), age creeping in, love oozing out, and hair falling off, keeps humans on their toes. That's why they never have time for anything!

As you grow, time turns into continuity, then continuity into a stable eternity without margins or horizons. Time becomes like the freeway—it's always there, and people hurry up and down, coming and going, changing vehicles but always on the freeway. So, first of all, a certain serenity pervades one. In equanimous inner silence, without judging or evaluating, something quite universal begins to appear: Everything on this earth seems to strive upward. Everything grows, even crystals. Each blade of grass thrusts upward, each sequoia tree, the chick and the elephant too, and this seemingly crazy humanity with houses and high rises, space shuttles and satellites, everything physically or morally strives to go up. And even if some dig downward for gold or oil, it is to finally rise, with their possessions, above their peers.

As we persevere and receive light through our inner powers, a general plan majestically opens up around us, like an apotheosis of light and love. Love and power of life. Oh, it's not an individual love born from desire, desire to possess, or even the motherly desire to protect. It is a cosmic, impersonal, all-embracing love, which seems to comprehend the tears and pains of growth, the birth pains of the species. We then understand this is the Will, the great Will toward liberation from the enslavement of form—form, which is the limitation of our essence, the fall into a thousand defined limits, just as molten, dazzling gold enters into the mold and freezes into immobility.

We are the creators, we are participating in this Will for freedom. We see its reflection in millions of human souls, so reduced, so belittled by the individual debility and fear of dissolution; but it is there. It masquerades in petty political comedies, historical dramas, ideals, flags, massacres; but it is always present in the heart of the social slave and the heart of the prophet.

In the last chapter we talked about our identity with the four elements of the cosmos, the gods among us: water, fire, earth, air. Let's take this a step further.

Our trouble is, we identify with our human problems. Lack, for instance. We lack health, we lack money, we lack an understanding partner. But remember, you do not exist as such, you are but a cloud of atoms. Only when you focus are you in this world. So identify with that within you that is not human. The elements never have any problems—they lack nothing. The elements are free. When we enter into their state of consciousness, when we recognize that we are them, we become free, and we too, lack nothing.

Of course as humans in our society, we will say, "Wait! What about money, homes, food, vehicles? The elements need none of these, but we have to possess them in order to survive." Of course we do! However, an attitude of "lacks" is actually very detrimental to our material gain as it *constricts*. It does not expand consciousness, which we need to do in order to attract favorable currents for success. That's why feeling the evidence of the elements, such as air blowing freely through our atomic formation—the one we visualize as a shape-limited individuality—will uplift our vision of the world and permit us to step out boldly on our way.

All that is not these elements, all that is human is an accumulation of conditioned automatisms. Feeling akin to the elements is power, the ability to extend into forms around us, to be part of everything. This co-vibration, or syntony, is love. This power is for service.

When we have lost the sense of duality, we are linked to all humans, to all living beings, visible or invisible, in one unique constitutional communion. *They are us; we are them.*

The natural desire to avoid suffering or low vibrations and darkness creates a craving toward high vibrations, light, and happiness. But obtaining this light creates a *responsibility* toward those remaining in darkness.

Empowerment gives birth to responsibility, as one always has to reckon with a newly acquired force. This responsibility is *to serve.* In every action you can find a thread of service. When you become more and more aware of this, you will discover the service in whatever you are doing.

Service is the way "up," a way to be part of the thrust of everything that grows. You can construct a ladder with the golden thread of service and be part of the thrust.

We need to serve where we find ourselves. To go off into a cave alone is to go back three thousand years. Rather, serve at home, in the urban jungle, wherever you are.

And don't try to keep track of your service, like a taxi meter. Nobody is counting "up there." Every time you do a service it is an immortal act, you are going with the upward thrust. It is just a childish belief that there is a celestial accountant who adds up your good deeds, just as your mother added quarters to your piggybank when you did what was expected of you. What happens is this: Every time you give—whatever—you expand your consciousness, you decondense, and go one slight step up the frequency scale towards light.

You don't need to identify with the service, or speak about it. Better to keep your mouth shut and just guide, love, care. And here's good news: If you expect opportunities for service, more will come—higher, easier ones.

Silence is a great aid in service. The more you are able to listen, the greater help you can be—energy escapes you when you talk. And when you have achieved serenity, you will benefit others by your mere presence. When your inner noise is silenced, you will have a quick, clear perspective on all human situations; you will be able to reach out effectively in generosity and compassion.

Compassion

Once you have climbed all the steps and achieved the tower of inner silence, you will see down there below the powerful, the violent, the learned, and the fools, all clamoring for attention. But look closely. They are only children, children wearing masks. The generals and clowns, presidents and godfathers, all made out of the mold of Homo sapiens, with their limitations, dreams, and final death. Thrown into the constant cosmic law of eternal recycling, their components processed through pain, rare joys, and tears, without the thread of memory that would save them from their lapse of oblivion, they constantly reappear like the leaves on trees, to fall and be trampled on in autumn.

It is from your inner silence, sturdily established through empowerment, and serene peace, that the flower of compassion will finally blossom. Compassion is not pity. The word comes from the Latin *cum*, meaning with, and the Greek *pathos*, suffering. It means to *suffer with*. This state of consciousness is the result of a very definite growth. Born from the vision of the wise, it will replace judgment and emotional craving for human justice.

What is there to judge? What is there to condemn? Our fathers and mothers were what they were. Our grandparents and great grandparents, too, down through the genealogical tree. Every cell, every movement of the blood, every synapse of the brain, have been building up circumstances that have brought us to this place, in this time, in these conditions, with our lives interwoven with others who are also in the same condition. When these threads cross each other over or under and the colors clash, you can imagine a pattern on which millions of lives have been embroidered. The orbit of recycling is too vast for our earthly sight. But from a higher level of understanding, one can see how the pattern has become darker and darker.

Look at all the other threads, how they come in. Look at what is going to happen. So is there any possibility of judgment? When a disaster does happen, we are horrified; but it has been woven in, it was on a collision course, prepared through time immemorial. When we see our fellow humans trapped in an inevitable situation, inevitable because of their ignorance of the current of cosmic Will, this is where our compassion comes in.

Being compassionate is the basis for your humanity. Act, do, come and go, have fun, cry, do whatever your life is preparing you for, do whatever you feel is necessary for your manifestation. But when you have the tendency to judge, to condemn, bring your consciousness up to the level of compassion. For this world is indeed the Valley of Tears, and only through compassion and service will you raise yourself beyond the limitations, the negative participation. Only through cosuffering can you understand what another individual needs. It is through cosuffering that you can find—if you are aware and fundamentally detached from what is happening—how you can help your fellow human beings and raise their eyes toward the stars. And as long as you can bring another to ask the question "Why?" you have put one of your fellow beings on the path to wisdom.

For one who is prepared, for the Initiate, human lives appear and disappear like bubbles on boiling water. But from the majority below, in the Valley of Tears, there comes the question: "Why must we go through this hell if it is only to return from where we came? It seems a tragic hoax!"

But they ignore the mechanics. This is a condensed level—

maybe not the most condensed, but still sufficiently dense to create obstacles which, once we have learned to remove them, prove our adequacy to function on all other levels of cosmic reality. When you master the obstacles here, you will find no obstacles above. Ours is an obstructed universe, higher universes are much less. So, as the pearl diver kicks off from the sea bottom, holding his treasure, and rises to the sunlight above where he belongs, you will return to your essence, which is cosmic impersonal love.

THE HUB OF THE WHEEL

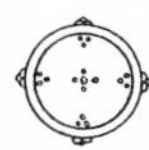

Even as from the waking state experience, there is no materiality in the objects seen in a dream (though while dreaming the objects appear to be solid), this world appears to be material yet in reality it is pure consciousness.

THE SUPREME YOGA

We are the mirror, as well as the face in it.
We are tasting the taste, this minute,
of Eternity. We are pain, and what cures pain, both.
We are the sweet cold water,
And the jar that pours.

RUMI

You are existing at many planes simultaneously at this moment. The only reason you don't know of your other identities is because you're so attached to this one . . . Go for broke, awake totally.

RAM DASS

You are that which you seek.

NISARGADATTA

Chapter 12

THE HUB OF THE WHEEL

The following explanation will give you a sort of "behind the scenes" vision of life and death. It may be fairly difficult to follow, but it will reward you with another vision, nearer to the kernel of the problem as humans see it.

Let us remember that everything we experience is done through our mind. We always think-feel. We always illustrate; we always localize. If we hear a sound, it is because our mind feels it, experiences it. The stimuli we receive we always dress up with thoughts, because we cannot think without images. Our thinking process developed with the organs of perception we were born with and ends with the deterioration of the organs at death, when *that* type of thinking is finished.

We also think in the astral level or dream world. The process of thinking surfaces at birth, our moment of condensation, and returns finally to where it always was, a sort of subconscious state of awareness—death. The blueprint of our mechanics is always present: the blueprint which every cell follows in forming the child; the blueprint of what becomes periodically, through recycling and through condensation, a brain, producing mental sensations again.

Now, try to find yourself at your highest possible level of thought and meditate on the following image:

When a movie projector shows a film, the rays of projection go through the air, which offers no opposition. Or they go through smoke in the room and we begin to see something because smoke acts as a screen. Then finally we see the rays on a wall or a screen, and there they acquire precision, angles, shapes, forms, and movement.

What has happened? When thought forms are projected through different condensations, objectivity is obtained because of *obstacle*. The projection of the film cannot go through the obstacle of the screen. On the screen we have objectivity, but in the smoke-filled room we have only vague pictures. That is a molecular level. The astral/molecular level is vague, fuzzy for those who are not sufficiently prepared, and lack the awareness to turn around and *recognize the projection as being theirs, from a center where all the film is already in the box.*

Think about this. The beginning of the film, the midpoint of the film, the end of the film; all of the phenomenon with its effects, its cause, its justice and injustice, its cruelty and its goodness: They are all in the little metal box. When this is projected through very thin air nothing is perceivable; in the smoky room it begins to be visible; and, hitting a very condensed level, it becomes real. But what reality has it except its own dynamics where time and space are created? In itself, the reel of film already had in it the beginning, the middle, and the end, happy or unhappy.

So this is what we must conceive as the hub of the wheel of *samsara*—the wheel of life and death. From the hub the spokes come out and sustain the rim in constant rotation. This state of being, this hub from where the projection is made, makes every different level of interruption of the rays of projection different *realities*. One is fuzzy, the land of shadows. One is precise: We call it real. But reality is neither one nor the other nor a third. The reality is up there in the metal box where the beginning and the end are *coexistent*, therefore simultaneous.

Our rational machine has great difficulty in understanding something that has no beginning and end. And this reel of ours is an endless loop, so it *has* no beginning. The beginning is nowhere. The end is nowhere. It is like the stars: Which is the central star of the cosmos? The center is everywhere, the circumference nowhere. This is our situation.

Please meditate at the center, at the hub of the wheel, the eternal loop, which is ever present in all aspects. Remember that the film projection presents objectivity only when it hits an obstacle. The smoke or mist catches part and lets the rest go through it: fuzzy vision. The whitewashed wall or screen lets nothing pass. Everything then seems real at that level. Try to understand: You are not at the level of the wall, but you can look at it. You are not at the level of the smoky mist that becomes a sort of mobile screen. *You are at the center of the projection, motionless, projecting the experience of the cosmos.*

For the moment do not try to find out *why*. You will get mixed up through your rational maze. The significance of this eternal why is that it brings us in touch with a part of the human experience which we might rather call prehuman. Some of it can only be "felt," not analyzed—for example, as expressed by the symbolism of the East in the ancient saga of the Dream of Brahman. The legend points to the Day and Night of Brahman which, though it lasts for a *kalpa* (4,300 million years), is but a blink of an eye for eternity. This brief dream is the period of *our* manifestation. When Brahman awakens, it vanishes as does "the early morning mist in the glorious light of the rising Sun." In other words, it never existed!

In order to put things together further, we also now have to listen with new ears to our western legend about the tragic fall of the Archangel. *This never was a fall.* It was a conscious plunge, a willful plunge by the bearer of light, Lucifer—who is subsequently called the arrogant, the defying Archangel, he who dares to challenge the divine law. In the legend Lucifer represents our human soul in rebellion against constant manifestation and recycling, against "following the rhythm of the Lord"—which echoes the *kalpas* and eons of Brahman's Dream.

Lucifer plunged to the condensations where he could work with obstacles towards freedom, in order not to reappear again and again—to become greater than the gods who had freed themselves from the limitations of form, but not from recycling. However, throughout our millenia of continual suffering, only a few, the "willing," have emerged eternal and free, to extend their compassion to their brothers and sisters still lost in the midst of illusion.

When one of the willing finally attains the level of cosmic unity, he justifies—we can say sanctifies—in that one instant of his enlightenment, the millions of souls without whom he would not have appeared on Earth. Rich or poor, humble or powerful, they would have lived, loved, and cried in vain if this last branch of their genealogical tree had not, thriving from their accumulated sum of joys, hopes and sorrows, brought to light the flower of liberation. As a thunderbolt strikes in one instant, in that very second all the links of this chain of human beings, up to then just an anonymous crowd, are redeemed of all *karma,* in whatever state of manifestation they might be in their cycle of returns. All their actions, loves, or crimes, up to then seemingly produced by blind passions, are totally and eternally justified as the unavoidable building blocks in this birth of a liberated being.

When you have passed through the door of inner silence, you may contemplate, from the highest summit of Intuition—and only from that level—the panorama of human suffering and the Luciferic plunge. Then you will receive the final answer to the eternal question of the spiritualist: "Why must I go through this hell, if it is only to return from where I came?"

And the answer vibrates through the cosmos with the splendor of evidence: "If I can be master of this condensation of energy—if I can lift a great weight, I can of course lift a much lighter one—I will be free from the limitations of the gods and their cycles. Then I can serve, transmute, and enlighten."

This is the meaning of the legends. It is through the loftiness of their symbols that we can *feel* what we do not clearly *see* at our rational level.

Now let us come down to this rational level again, to the explanation of the projection. The important part is to feel yourself at the center, at the *lens,* observing the different situations at different levels of condensation, realizing you can go down to the wall, enjoy the picture, still realizing it is a very relative way of perceiving.

Free yourselves of the illusion of objectivity as a reality. It is one of the many realities. We live in each of them, but *simultaneously.* We feel and live and experience these different realities at the same time.

If you have a tendency to forget, remember just one vision: The reel that contains the movie in all its details is complete. What is thrown is a projection which will be opposed at each different condensation until finally it is stopped at the wall or screen, a condensation of atoms that will not let the photons go through. Remember: The projection is the same manifestation at different levels. None is more real than another. A wall is as real as a smoke screen, each one in its own right. We experience each one according to our focus on each one. Keep this in mind and you will have made a step ahead in the dissolution of objectivity and recognition of yourself at different levels of existence.

The following will make our mental limitations clear: We all live, act and experience *simultaneously,* as I explained earlier. We can drive, look, admire, eat candy, talk shop, hold the hand of a dear person, hear music, and smell the ocean air—all at the same time. But as you see, I must take time when I want to describe it, because my reason, with which I think, *cannot* in any way give me a simultaneous image. It can only think in sequence, like the frames of a film. How imposible to imagine that the end of a war exists before it began! We cannot understand it anymore than we can lift ourselves by our belts into the middle of the room. The mechanics of the thinking process do not allow it, and we can only think by abiding to the mechanics of the machine, just as we can only typewrite according to the mechanics of the typewriter.

Still, keep it in your consciousness as a possibility, as maybe a reality that you will constantly and furiously doubt. That's fine. Reason *throws* itself against these things and that is what it should do, proving to itself its capacity to resist in its medium. Nevertheless, when we finally attain that state of consciousness when the "drop of water" (the "I am") absorbs in its consciousness the "ocean" (the cosmos itself), then even our mind can understand that expansion of movement through duration (space and time) is meaningless. Why does it appear here in the 3-D world? Because of the instrument that receives cosmic impulses and translates, filters, and organizes them like a computer, only within its own limits.

This is sometimes a heartbreaking vision. We do love to think we can influence those cosmic impulses at the level of their manifestation. But any change can only be made at the hub of the wheel, just as any change on the film can only be made at the time of shooting it. Later, whatever the "obstacle" you project it upon, the story will be the same.

So consider this as a possibility beyond rational understanding, and then it will appear to you that there is a way which, in constant synthesis after synthesis, will absorb all the differences that we still see as cause and effect in one overwhelming state of being: "I Am The One That Is."

EPILOG

Be at peace within with a steady mind. Rest in the inner silence. Be free from all mental perversions and from the blinding taint of illusion. Rest content in your own self. Remain in an expansive state in the self, like the full ocean.

THE SUPREME YOGA

Walk fearlessly, eating what you must, growing wherever you can, like the monk on the road who knows precisely how vulnerable he is, who takes no comfort among death-forgetting men, and who carries his vision of vastness and might around in his tunic like a live coal which neither burns nor warms him, but with which he will not part.

ANNIE DILLARD

His thought is quiet, quiet are his word and deed, when he has obtained freedom by true knowledge, when he has thus become a quiet man.

BUDDHA

If water derives lucidity from stillness, how much more the faculties of the mind! The mind of the sage, being in repose, becomes the mirror of the universe.

CHUANG TZU

EPILOG

I want to shake up your concepts of reality, but I do not mean to give the impression that there is nothing out there. On the contrary, there's a lot out there. But by shifting from the perceptions of our five senses to multidimensional perceptions, we can propel our consciousness through many levels.

Take the ocean, for example. You can see it, smell it, taste it, touch it, hear it—the five senses are all involved. You perceive it this way, just as water. But if you could perceive it as an energy field, if you had another sense that would be impacted by the energy field of the ocean, what would happen then? You would immediately, if you plugged yourself into this ocean of energy, *be* the whole oceanic magnetic field and electronic vibrating energy. You would then, at the speed of light, perceive and know and be everything in its totality, as far as the ocean is concerned.

"It doesn't work," you will say. "I am still sitting on this cushion. I can feel it, so my body hasn't budged. All this talking about going beyond our sensory barrier is just a game of imagination."

Let me try to dissolve this mental feedback for you: The physical body is only perceived as such because of two specific conditions.

First, our scale of observation, conditioned by the limits of our senses, which are part of the body. From any microbe's point of view, the human body would be seen as a gigantic formation, with immense proportional distances between the atoms that construct it.

Second, the energy fields that compose the physical body are quite varied. Although divided (flesh, bones, blood), they overlap at the margins. And when the main currents, like the mental and the emotional, are drawn towards a different focus, the totality is affected. Some of it follows suit, stretches in the same direction. The whole is a sort of fluid body, of which one part goes in a direction, and pulls a great quantity of the rest.

The main objection—that the body doesn't budge and therefore the experiences are unreal—smacks of our old materialistic concepts, that dimensions are "traveled" and therefore include the category of space. The term "travel" is a form of speech taken from Theosophical teachings. In fact, no travel has to happen. The whole dynamic takes place as a *change of frequencies,* in which you may tune into any other syntonic level.

Let us pause a moment and look back down at where we started. During our efforts it was not easy to look back, but now we can measure the distance from our starting point.

The world, the solid world of ordinary people, has crumbled and vanished into fields of energy, thinner than a morning mist. What about us? Fields of energy in the vibrating cosmos, we have abandoned our strife against matter, this nonexistent abstraction, a nightmare of ignorance. Although we are still sensitive and aware of our bodies, we feel that our relation to this world is a matter of syntony, of being in tune, of tuning in to communicate, of knowing we *are.*

Perhaps we still hesitate, not fully confident of the new evidence. This is because Reason is only slowly giving up its command, yielding its place to more subtle impulses, retreating to its position among its three-dimensional creations. Believe me, this is a victory. It is, of course, only the beginning, but we are already folding the map and contemplating the journey. Let us remember that Reason grows and multiplies its circuits as we evolve.

I also realize that the panorama you are confronting is somewhat breathtaking, and may be frightening for some. But why not face it? Homo sapiens is obsolete—as obsolete as the dinosaurs. Most of our principles do not work—even the famous Big Stick policy, which we can no longer handle without destroying stage, scenery, and actors. Our moral values are most of the time for decorative purposes, taught to children but never applied.

The new species is appearing. You are and should be part of it. And the transmutation can take place while you are still alive and active. It is a question of powerful will—your will becomes the cosmic Will. Destiny guides you.

We have been dissolving the components of our incarnation, slowly cutting the fetters that bind us to this human experience. And now we stand in a world of inner silence, devoid of color or form. The slightest parting of our atoms would turn the sense of touch into a mere abstraction. What separates us from immateriality is just a magnetic cohesion!

Nevertheless, we recognize our thoughts, sentiments, emotions as our own. We're still the same—we know we have not changed, qualitatively. But in this inner silence we shall begin to receive subtle messages that do not come through the channels of the senses which we have silenced at will, along with the concept of solid matter. The message is the voice of silence, contact with the countless other dimensions of the cosmos, the union from within with divinity.

However, if our world is just an illusion, our bodies another, this question arises: "Composed of aggregates accumulated through millions of generations, conditioned to think, feel, and act, hurtling through an imaginary world like a water spout in a tornado, made of fragments picked up on the way and vanishing when the energy retreats, *who am I*—if all I can recognize as 'me' has just been dissolved into nothingness?"

That, my friend, is the last question. No intellectual effort can ever satisfy it. Because Reason, the instrument whose limits are the cause of the question, cannot find an answer that lies in another dimension.

There is only one way. That is to become, in your totality, the answer. To *be*, instead of merely to *exist* through the constant rhythms of thoughts and blank moments, days and blind nights, life and mysterious death. To be, through your own action.

To the definition of godhood which I have given you, I now add my parting gift. May these two unique explanations light your path and guide you on your way. What follows is to help you grasp the actual process of enlightenment, for this is where I am leading you, if you are among the willing.

There is only one way to enlightenment. It is through the "hot line" that the messages from the subtle levels will be translated into *understanding.* As we persevere with inner development, as we continue to grow and expand, our awareness intensifies to the point of becoming a vehicle itself, which tends to manifest in ever more subtle levels of energy. Maybe this will happen during our lifetime because of our unceasing efforts, maybe at the transition of death. When at last we are able to go beyond form, we will realize that even light is still a form and has to be discarded. But this only happens at the moment of final transmutation.

Light is the essence of everything on the physical level of our planet. Yes, everything. Even the black plastic pen I am writing with is the result of light, through a petrochemical transformation: oil and coal from vegetable life nourished by sunlight. Wherever we look, from the fiery lava of our mineral world to the evaporating seas, all is light. And light is life-giving love.

One can only enter/become light if one has grown beyond duality, to be of its *same quality.* This means to become its essence, the cosmic impersonal divine love and life-giving force, thus bringing about the incredible happening, the silent cosmic explosion of transmutation from existence. In one great burst of superhuman joy and infinite bliss, the seeker, now the divine essence of life, becomes the universe, and the universe becomes the seeker.

From here on, no words can define the limitless; we can only plunge through contemplation into the fathomless depth of symbols.

INVOCATION

I have shed the thirst for attachment,
The hunger for consoling illusions,
The fear and sadness of solitude.

I take into my heart my parents,
for now I am the father and mother.
I take into my heart my children,
for now I am their crown of glory.
I take into my heart the world,
for now I justify its existence.

Beyond form, beyond the gods, "I am,"
the formless, the silence, the eternal . . .

Some time ago, you opened this book. Now look back at the first page. You have left it far behind, for you have already entered the door to Inner Silence.

ABOUT THE AUTHOR

Andrew Da Passano's highly colorful life began November 22, 1905, in St. Petersberg, Russia. His father was the Marquis Eugenio Da Passano; his mother was Elizabeth Soltikoff, daughter of the writer Soltikoff Schedrin, who is still greatly admired in Russia. At that time the Marquis Da Passano represented the Electric Boat and Submarine Corporation of Newark—in Czarist Russia and also in the far East and Europe. Andrew traveled extensively with his father, later serving as his secretary. In the process, he learned and practiced the six languages that he speaks fluently today.

The Da Passano family, whose castle was built on the highest peak overlooking Genoa, were developers of the Republic of Genoa, and the Da Passano name, dating from 960 A.D., is still engraved in the most important historical monuments, buildings, and churches of the city. Through the centuries, during the wars with Venice for the supremacy of the Mediterranean trade, many of the leaders of the family came in contact with the East, and the Crusades left a deep imprint in the family tradition.

During his early years, Andrew had a weak physical body, but he was constantly in touch with a reality incomprehensible to his parents: the dimension beyond physical forms. He experienced nightly instances of clairaudience: sublime music, which began at precisely the same moment every night and lasted for an hour. This went on until he was eleven.

Later, through the practice of swimming, wrestling, and boxing, he developed his physical body. Throughout this development, though, he always felt the guidance of European warrior consciousnesses he identified as belonging to his family past.

Life for Andrew remained very pleasant while his father was "in the money." The family bought the Anchorage Estate in Long Branch, New Jersey, from the banker Bernard Baruch, and they had a large villa in Monaco. In Paris they lived in an apartment once owned by Talleyrand, the minister of Napoleon.

In the Depression, however, the Marquis Da Passano lost his fortune and died of a heart attack in Paris in 1930. Difficult times began for Andrew. He was forced to develop his proficiency as a commercial artist in order to survive. In Paris he worked as a dress designer and decorator for the *Follies Bergere* at the *Casino de Paris*. He created stage decorations for Mistinguette at the *Moulin Rouge*. In Germany, he worked on stage design. He ran a lampshade studio in Chelsea, London.

Through all these changes he remained on his spiritual quest and in 1938 he met his spiritual teacher, Tulio Castellani. After some years of study Andrew cofounded with him the Center of Spiritual Culture in Milan, which continues to function actively today.

As it did with everyone, World War II greatly changed Andrew's life. Using his knowledge of submarine weaponry, he developed the acoustic torpedo for his own country, Italy, later gaining the rank of captain in the Italian navy. War brought him personal tragedy: during the August 1943 air raid on Milan, he lost his only child of two, who died in his arms.

The suffering from this loss drove him to intensify his inner development. Andrew plunged with new fervor into rigorous spiritual exercises and study with Castellani. Castellani, known as "The Venetian," was a no-nonsense teacher who didn't indulge his pupils. One day during meditation, the fragrance of white roses came to Andrew. He opened his eyes and saw the Buddha – clear and real. Tremendously excited, he hurried by train and on foot for many miles through wartime Milan to tell his teacher the great news.

The only response was: "Fine. And did you do your exercises?"

Toward the end of the war, Andrew joined the Italian partisans to fight against the Nazis, worked with the Red Cross, and finally joined the Allied troops. After the war, he became a publisher in

Milan and a successful artist in Paris.

He was invited by UNESCO to undertake an educational program to combat illiteracy in Mexico. Once there, he stayed and taught for twenty-five years, establishing in 1954 the Center of Initiatic Culture in Mexico City, which still continues under his direction, with a branch in Guadalajara. It was in 1956 that he experienced self-realization, which he refers to as his "revelation." He continued to teach, to try to bring others to the same transcendant moment. From 1961 to 1965, he was a professor at the University of Guadalajara. And in 1977 he moved to Los Angeles, California.

Through he is now in his eighties, Andrew is not the sort of man who retires. He continues to teach, and his students are of different ages and professions — stockbrokers, artists, college students, attorneys, actors, writers. Although the school is deeply traditional, it is adapted to Western mentality. Andrew's broad knowledge encompasses today's most advanced theoretical science, which dovetails with the ancient wisdom of the East. From the Eastern philosophies, particularly Tibetan Buddhism and Taoism, Andrew presents techniques that until recently were part of a secret oral tradition. It's an eclectic system, both esoteric and highly practical, which explains the name of his school in Los Angeles, the Temple of Esoteric Science — secret traditions combining with the latest knowledge to create a new vision.

He is currently married to his fourth wife, Virginia Da Passano of Mexico, a doctor of Oriental medicine. When Andrew is not writing books or keeping up with his young grandson, he gives weekly classes and seminars at his school in addition to a regular cable television program. Never the guru on a pedestal, Andrew is accessible, always available when a student faces a life crisis. He's a dedicated teacher and a compassionate friend.

Imagine that the grey-bearded Merlin has returned with all his powers and wisdom intact, that he is youthful and energetic with a wry sense of humor, that he now talks about quantum physics and the Buddha. This may give you a picture of Andrew.